Also by Gabrielle Giffords and Mark Kelly:

Gabby: A Story of Courage and Hope

ENOUGH

OUR FIGHT TO KEEP AMERICA SAFE FROM GUN VIOLENCE

Gabrielle Giffords and Mark Kelly

with Harry Jaffe

SCRIBNER

New York London Toronto Sydney New Delhi

Scribner
A Division of Simon & Schuster, Inc.
1230 Avenue of the Americas
New York, NY 10020

First Scribner hardcover edition October 2014

SCRIBNER and design are registered trademarks of The Gale Group, Inc.,
used under license by Simon & Schuster, Inc., the publisher of this work.

For information about special discounts for bulk purchases,
please contact Simon & Schuster Special Sales at 1-866-506-1949
or business@simonandschuster.com.

The Simon & Schuster Speakers Bureau can bring authors to your live event.
For more information or to book an event, contact the Simon & Schuster Speakers
Bureau at 1-866-248-3049 or visit our website at www.simonspeakers.com.

Interior design by Erich Hobbing
Jacket design by Eric White
Jacket photographs: front © *The Washington Post*/Contributor/Getty Images;
back © Eric Elofson (Revolution Messaging)

Manufactured in the United States of America

1   3   5   7   9   10   8   6   4   2

Library of Congress Cataloging-in-Publication Data is available.

ISBN 978-1-4767-5007-1
ISBN 978-1-4767-5011-8 (ebook)

In memory of

Charlotte Bacon
Daniel Barden
Rachel D'Avino
Olivia Engel
Josephine Gay
Dawn Hochsprung
Dylan Hockley
Madeleine IIsu
Catherine Hubbard
Chase Kowalski
Jesse Lewis
Ana Márquez-Greene
James Mattioli
Grace McDonnell
Anne Marie Murphy
Emilie Parker
Jack Pinto
Noah Pozner
Caroline Previdi
Jessica Rekos
Avielle Richman
Lauren Rousseau
Mary Sherlach
Victoria Soto
Benjamin Wheeler
Allison Wyatt

CONTENTS

ENOUGH

INTRODUCTION

We are a reasonable people, we Americans. We share common goals: life, liberty, and the pursuit of happiness. Those words have knit us together since 1776. They spelled out who we were then. They are just as uplifting and foundational today.

Our diversity has made us a bigger-hearted people. Regardless of our religion or skin color or political allegiances, we are all Americans, and we come together to root for our favorite sports teams and watch fireworks on July 4. We vote and we pay taxes, and we send our kids to school every morning with the expectation that they'll return to us that night safe, happy, and maybe a little smarter.

We have remained intact, weathering the inevitable disagreements of a strong democracy, for over two hundred years, through wars and peacetime, recessions and prosperity, struggles over civil rights and equality.

But Gabby and I fear the country has veered off course when it comes to one important issue: how we relate to guns. A basic freedom that both Gabby and I wholeheartedly embrace, the right to bear arms, has become radicalized.

When guns get in the hands of the wrong people, as has happened all too often in recent years, they can transform even the safest places—a movie theater, a place of worship, a school, a shopping center—into combat zones. More and more over the past decades, guns have not only been used to keep the peace, but to rob us of our peace.

Gabby and I came face-to-face with the most horrific aspects of America's gun-violence problem on the morning of January 8, 2011. As Gabby was meeting with constituents in a Tucson shopping center, a young man wielding a semi-automatic handgun shot her in the head at close range. In fewer than fifteen seconds, he murdered six people, including Arizona's chief federal judge and a nine-year-old girl, and wounded sixteen others.

* * *

For the next two years, the most basic life-or-death questions consumed our family: Would Gabby survive the bullet through her brain? Would she walk again? Smile that smile that won my heart? Speak? Hug her friends?

Miraculously—but with great difficulty and much painful work—Gabby has prevailed over the injury to her brain. We have shared joy and frustration, wins and losses along the way. Doctors, friends, family, and Americans everywhere helped us through the hardest moments, and they remain essential to my wife's continued well-being.

All along the way, Gabby's ongoing recovery has compelled us to ask larger questions that confront us as a nation, and time and time again we returned to the subject of guns.

What can we do to protect innocent Americans from the mass shootings that have become so commonplace in the years before and after Gabby was shot in Tucson? These tragedies are forever imprinted in our national consciousness: Virginia Tech, Aurora, Newtown, the Washington Navy Yard, Fort Hood—and these are only recent examples.

INTRODUCTION

Mass shootings, however, mask the toll of everyday gun violence that is horrifying in its banal frequency. More than thirty-one thousand Americans died by gunfire in 2010, over a third of these homicides. Add nonfatal wounds, and you have a national nightmare—one that makes our country stand out in the worst ways. The US rate of firearm homicide for children ages five to fourteen is thirteen times higher than in any other developed nation. Our gun-murder rate is about fifteen to twenty times the average of countries like France, Italy, Japan, and the United Kingdom.

Why does this keep happening? Why are we just sitting back and watching while more and more innocent Americans lose their lives to gun violence?

Gabby and I started to wonder if perhaps reasonable people—the overwhelming majority of us, after all—might be able to band together to make our country less dangerous. We began to ask ourselves: What can we do to keep guns out of the hands of people who cannot be trusted with firearms? How can we preserve the rights of law-abiding citizens to own guns for hunting and self-protection while keeping them away from criminals and the dangerously mentally ill?

How can we give law enforcement the tools it needs to stop guns from being traded illegally by unscrupulous dealers? To bring criminals to justice by tracing guns used in crimes, and to make it harder for known stalkers and domestic abusers to acquire guns?

* * *

After Tucson and the shootings that have followed, Gabby and I have returned to these questions again and again. She and I had dedicated our lives to public service, out of love and duty. Our work is not yet done.

Gabby entered politics in 2000 when she was elected to the Arizona House of Representatives. Then, at just thirty-two, she became the youngest woman elected to the Arizona Senate. The voters of Tucson and Arizona's Eighth Congressional District elected her to Congress in 2006. They reelected her in 2008 and 2010. As Congress convened on January 6, 2011, Gabby read the First Amendment of the Constitution on the House floor. Two days later, she was shot in the head.

I joined the United States Navy and started flight school in 1986 in Pensacola. I qualified as a sharpshooter while at the US Merchant Marine Academy and later as an expert marksman in the Navy. I flew thirty-nine combat missions over Iraq and Kuwait in the first Gulf War. I went on to become a test pilot and then an astronaut, piloted two space shuttle missions and commanded two more, and spent more than fifty days in space.

After the Tucson shooting, Gabby and I kept discussing different paths of public service we might pursue. No matter where the conversation started, we found that we inevitably returned to the same subject: gun violence.

* * *

Now, Gabby and I had never had any quarrel with the Second Amendment: "A well-regulated militia, being necessary to the security of a free state, the right of the people to keep and bear arms, shall not be infringed."

My wife and I have always believed deeply in that principle, and we see no need to infringe on that right. We are proud to be among the 34 percent of American households that reported owning guns in 2012. I occasionally hunt. Gabby has owned a handgun for years. She shot with her right hand before the shooting disabled her right side; these days, she's learning to shoot with her left hand.

But as much as we love guns, we also believe in the rule of law. Because we care about public safety, we don't allow people to drive cars on the sidewalk, and we don't permit teenagers to buy alcohol, and we take measures to ensure that our kids aren't drinking arsenic in the school water fountain. Why, then, can't we agree on a few simple rules about gun ownership that honor the Second Amendment while protecting Americans from random gun violence?

In the last two decades, anyone who's dared ask that sensible question has been muzzled by intransigent and uncompromising political interest groups, most notably the National Rifle Association. The NRA's response to any question about tightening restrictions on gun ownership is a resounding "No!" Though only about 1.5 percent of Americans are members, the NRA has the money and political might to rank among the most powerful interest groups in the nation.

The NRA began as a venerable organization of gun owners but has since diverged from its founding principles—and also from its own membership. Does the average card-carrying NRA member know that the organization is actually a trade association that's more focused on corporate profits than the rights of gun owners? The NRA's stated mission is to "protect and defend the Constitution"—but they also make time for generating revenues of almost $228 million a year. A regular annual NRA membership costs thirty-five dollars; the top brass at the NRA, like its CEO Wayne LaPierre, take home nearly a million a year.

Instead of protecting the interests of the law-abiding gun owners who dominate their membership rolls, NRA leaders increasingly sound as if they're advocating turning our country into an armed camp. After a deranged gunman murdered twenty-six people, including twenty young children, at Sandy Hook Elementary in Newtown, Connecticut, in December 2012, LaPierre's only suggestion was that we station armed security guards in every school—a measure that we don't necessarily oppose, but we certainly don't think it's enough to protect our kids. As LaPierre is fond of saying, "The only thing that stops a bad guy with a gun is a good guy with a gun."

Really?

So where will it end? Will we arm teachers and soccer coaches, too? Parents who chaperone class trips to the zoo? Preachers, ministers, and rabbis? I just cannot imagine my second-grade teacher stashing a pistol in the pocket of the pink muumuu that she wore most days.

The NRA has, in essence, turned the tables on the Declaration of Independence. Forget about a government designed to protect "life, liberty and the pursuit of happiness." Most of us trust our government: even if, sure, the average ninth grader can build a better website, we believe that the men and women we elect to represent us have our best interests at heart. But to hear the NRA tell it, once federal or state governments start to pass laws to reduce gun violence in *any* way, shape, or form, it's a "slippery slope" to "jackbooted" federal agents banging on a gun owner's door to demand he turn over his firearm.

As a Navy pilot who risked his life during bombing missions over Iraq and Kuwait, I find that preposterous and offensive. I was fighting to protect the ideals of a country and a government that I believed in. I blasted into space for my country, in a government-financed spaceship. The NRA's slippery slope is a fantasy, and a dangerous one. If the NRA gets its way, we'll be left with a country where everyone is armed but no one is safe.

"Nonsense," Gabby says of the NRA's crusade to prevent the government from passing laws about who should be able to get their hands on guns. She came within an inch of death while she was performing her basic duty in a representative democracy—meeting with constituents. As a gun owner, she would have been safer if we'd established some basic rules to keep guns away from men and women with severe mental illnesses like the one who shot her and murdered six of her constituents and staff.

We need to do more to protect our citizens from these horrific acts of violence that have become all too common in our society.

*   *   *

Together with friends and supporters, we answered the call to stand up for reasonable, rational responses to gun violence. In early 2013, on the two-year anniversary of the Tucson shooting, we created Americans for Responsible Solutions, an organization devoted to protecting Americans and helping to change our laws. Our initial goals are simple:

- To create an environment where people with different viewpoints can finally get down to discussing these crucial issues. Let's replace the inflammatory rhetoric on both sides of this debate (and yes, that very much includes those coastal liberals who reflexively demonize the culture of guns without understanding it) with a real exchange of ideas.
- To change the politics of this debate, so that gun laws are

7

no longer strictly a partisan issue—and so that elected officials are no longer cowed into voting against the will of their constituents.

- To work toward some moderate, commonsense policy shifts that the overwhelming majority of Americans supports: expanding background checks, coming to the aid of women who seek protection from abusive partners with firearms, combating illegal gun trafficking, and improving the background-check system with better records reporting.

Gabby and I share a hopeful vision for America. We believe in each other, in our communities, in our countrymen, in our nation. We are committed to building an organization that will stand for those values and also uphold the right to bear arms established in the Bill of Rights. We can do both.

We aren't naïve. We know that achieving our goals will require compromise, patience, and a tremendous amount of work. But that's fine: the two of us are in this for the long haul.

Americans are fed up with the gun violence ripping apart our communities. It's time we did something about it.

CHAPTER ONE

THE LINE
IN THE SAND

G abby and I never imagined we'd be working alongside each other, day in, day out, on a single issue like reducing gun violence.

When Gabby and I first met and fell in love, she was a rising star in Arizona politics and headed toward three successful runs for Congress representing a district stretching across southeastern Arizona. She lived in Tucson when she wasn't in Washington. I was an astronaut working out of Houston when I wasn't in space. Sometimes we would do the circuit clockwise—DC to Houston to Tucson—and sometimes counterclockwise—Tucson to Houston to Washington, DC. We were in constant motion. It was a complicated arrangement, but we had settled into a routine.

This routine was shattered when Gabby was shot on January 8, 2011. For months afterward we spent our lives in hospitals, doctors' offices, and a rehabilitation center. Gabby survived her traumatic brain injury, and, slowly but surely, began to recover.

On May 16, 2011, Gabby was well enough to fly to Florida and see me off for my final space shuttle mission and my second as commander. That June I retired from NASA, posting a message online: "From the day I entered the United States Merchant Marine Academy in the summer of 1982 to the moment I landed Space Shuttle *Endeavour* three weeks ago, it has been my privilege to advance the ideals that define the United States of America."

Seven months later, though she was making steady progress, Gabby decided to step down from Congress. A little more than a year after she was shot, we were both out of government service and ready to re-create our lives as private citizens, together.

*   *   *

Early on in her recovery, while staying at a rehabilitation hospital in Houston, Gabby felt a strong pull to get back to Tucson. Under the circumstances, I was ready to leave Houston, too. After years of commuting, our decision to stay in the same place was one small positive outcome of Gabby's injury. We agreed to move back to Tucson and began looking for houses in the summer of 2012.

Gabby loved the grittier parts of her hometown. She often referred to herself as "a woman of the people." When she returned to Tucson in 1996 to help manage her family's tire company, she chose to live in Barrio Viejo, a neighborhood near historic downtown Tucson.

"How about if we look in the foothills?" I asked.

"Not my style," she responded.

On one of my first house-hunting trips, I visited a house in a small development just east of the University of Arizona, near the Reid Park Zoo. I walked into a foyer with tile floors and stepped into a great room with vaulted ceilings, expansive walls, and a view to the pool in the backyard. To the left was this perfect kitchen with room for a table by the windows. To the right, down a hall, were three bedrooms. Gabby could navigate the place well. There were few steps. She could swim in the pool and take walks in the neighborhood.

I had a feeling Gabby would like this place.

That night Gabby came to check it out. She stepped inside, looked around, walked into the kitchen and out back to the pool. She seemed noncommittal. We had a way of communicating that didn't always require many words. Her eyes showed doubt, I thought.

"I have ten more houses I want to look at tomorrow," I said.

"No," she said. "This is it." What I had read as doubt was actually the glint of determination.

*　　*　　*

By August we were ready to move in, with plenty of help. Gabby's mom, Gloria, pitched in, along with our friend Suzy Gershman. We furnished the living room with knickknacks and furniture we had each accumulated over the years. We lined the shelves with our favorite books.

Those expansive walls provided plenty of space for paintings that formerly crowded the walls of Gabby's condo. There are few material objects that hold Gabby's interest. Paintings top the list, along with an old motorcycle and a couple of Vespa scooters that don't run anymore. Tucson artist Jim Waid had loaned two large paintings to Gabby for her congressional offices. One, a colorful splash of red flower petals and vines and orange peppers against a backdrop of blues and greens, had hung on her DC office wall until she resigned. Without telling Gabby, I bought both paintings and surprised her with them when we were in Houston. Now we hung one on the wall facing the family room and the other in the dining room. Above the fireplace, we placed a huge mural by Rudans, an artist who had once lived near Gabby in the barrio.

Nelson, Gabby's yellow Lab, swam in the pool and lounged on the cool stone patio. My younger daughter, Claire, moved in with us and enrolled in high school.

Once again, our lives fell into a nice routine. On most days I would rise before Gabby, drive Claire to school, then return to work at home. Since retiring from NASA and the Navy, I was consulting for an aerospace company and giving some speeches. I was also working on a couple of children's books. I was on the road a good amount, so I treasured my days in Tucson. Gabby and I would have breakfast together, and then I might take a hike in Sabino Canyon. We would cook dinner together and relax in front of the TV. I'm embarrassed to admit this, but we watched sixty-something episodes of *Glee* in a single month.

Gabby worked every day at breaking through barriers to her complete recovery. Physical therapy twice a week. Occupational therapy once a week. Speech therapy three times a week. She was constantly reading newspapers, books, and magazines. Communicating with friends, fans, and former constituents. Stretching. Walking twenty minutes or more every day. Doing yoga.

The bullet that passed through the left side of Gabby's brain caused significant paralysis to the right side of her body. She had no use of her right arm, and her right leg was mostly paralyzed. She had to learn to walk again. She learned to write and use her iPad with her left hand. The bullet wound robbed her of the ability to speak with ease, but she made steady—

and remarkable—progress. She still does, every single day. Her mind is clear, her memory intact, her thinking crisp.

I would often find her at the kitchen table working on Lumosity, a website with brain-training exercises and programs. She would run through a training routine. I would try the same one.

She would often outscore me.

*   *   *

On December 12, 2012, four months after moving to Tucson, I flew to Beijing.

A good friend had asked me to speak to his company in China. We had talked about Gabby coming along but decided against it. China is a special place for us. We met each other while traveling there in 2003 when we were both invited to attend a Young Leaders Forum of the National Committee on United States–China Relations. She was an Arizona state senator; I was in training as the pilot on my second space shuttle mission. We met during a layover in Vancouver, and as we were boarding the plane the next day she found me and asked: "Why don't we sit together?" Strapped in for twelve hours, we talked nonstop. After that trip, we didn't see each other for a year, but then Gabby had to visit death row at Florence State Prison, just outside of her district, and she couldn't find anyone to accompany her. I was always up for a new experience, and that's how we began dating. It's been quite the roller coaster ever since.

I was thinking of Gabby as I touched down in Beijing.

Jet-lagged and woozy from my travels, I had a fitful night's sleep in my hotel. By five o'clock the next morning, I gave up, powered on my phone, and turned on the TV to check the news. The first reports of a school shooting in Newtown, Connecticut, popped up. They described a scene of carnage in an elementary school. Dead children and teachers. I could not fathom the tragedy. I was incredulous. Not again.

My first call was to Gabby. It was eight P.M. in Tucson. "You've probably seen the news," I said.

I sat glued to CNN, absorbing every detail of the tragedy as it unfolded on the screen.

"Yes," she said. "Terrible. Terrible."

We traded information on what we were hearing in news reports: a lone gunman with a high-powered semiautomatic rifle had walked into a public elementary school and shot twenty children and six educators. We couldn't believe it had happened in the wake of so many other recent mass murders by gunfire: Virginia Tech, Tucson, Aurora.

"Now twenty first graders," I said.

"We must help," Gabby said.

"What do you mean?"

"Do something," she said. "Not just talk."

* * *

Though our plans crystallized in the aftermath of the Newtown shooting, Gabby and I had begun talking about taking action on gun laws months earlier. On July 21, 2012, we had flown to Europe for a two-week combined vacation and work trip. The day before we left, a gunman dressed in tactical clothing killed twelve and wounded fifty-eight others in a movie theater in Aurora, Colorado, during a midnight screening of the latest *Batman* film.

The shooting had cast a shadow over the trip. It was hard to think about anything else. On the plane, I turned to Gabby and said: "Let's put out a statement."

14

Gabby nodded, then shook her head. "Not enough," she said.

I agreed.

In the past, that was the expected protocol following one of these tragic shootings: you put out a statement mourning the victims and condemning gun violence while implicitly agreeing that "Now is not the time to talk about politics."

But maybe that was the wrong approach. Maybe now *was* the time to discuss the policies that allowed these massacres to keep happening. If not in the immediate aftermath, then when?

After Aurora, we released the expected statement, but we had both privately decided that enough was enough. Words alone would no longer cut it. We—or somebody—had to *do* something about the gun violence ripping so many communities apart. But what?

"We need to think about getting more involved in this issue," I said. "We can't just sit back and watch as these shootings keep happening."

"But how?" Gabby asked.

For much of the flight, we wrestled with our options. We could start an organization to advocate changes in gun laws. We might turn up the volume on our statements to the press. Or perhaps we could take a more direct, political route.

Politics came naturally to Gabby. She thrived in the public sphere and had a knack for connecting with people. In her years in the state legislature and Congress, she also learned how to play and win the bare-knuckle political games in the back rooms of Phoenix and Washington. She knew how to raise money. She knew the difference between the possible, the probable, and the improbable. She could count votes.

I could count the minutes and seconds it took for a space

shuttle to get into and out of Earth's orbit. Eight minutes and twenty-six seconds, to be exact, for *Endeavour*'s last trip into space.

Growing up the son of cops in a small New Jersey town, I wasn't all that interested in local or even national politics. I didn't even know if my parents were Republicans or Democrats, and in fact I *still* don't know. My mom passed away recently without ever clueing me in. She was always independent-minded—just like Gabby, who was a Republican in her twenties before becoming a moderate Democrat. My father, who has long since retired as a detective, is a political enigma. He watches Fox News continuously, though he'd dispute this; he claims it's just a coincidence that I only see him watching Fox. But every time I kid him about being a conservative Republican, he whips out a card in his wallet with his party affiliation and tells me: "I'm a Democrat!"

I'm still not convinced.

Gabby introduced me to retail politics. I was by her side as she ran for Congress. I watched her make decisions and weigh the pros and cons of policy positions or votes. She would consider what she thought was right, what her constituents wanted, who was making the loudest noise—and whether she should listen.

After a few years with Gabby, I had a much better understanding of how we make laws and why it was often compared to making sausage. It's not a pretty process. Gabby and I also lamented what seemed like politicians' inability to compromise on issues big and small. My wife's friends and colleagues in Congress had taken stands in stark opposition to one another, and the middle ground had become a no-man's-land.

"Too divided," Gabby would say.

Two weeks in Europe gave us a chance to relax and reflect. We can't say that our concerns over American gun laws occupied our every thought and conversation. But every once in a while, Gabby would catch my eye and say: "Aurora. Horrible. Happened again."

* * *

If Aurora started us talking, Newtown finally shocked us into taking action. The day of those unforgettable shootings, Gabby and I posted a statement on our Facebook pages that marked the internal shift we'd made from passive horror to active engagement. One part of the statement read, "As we mourn, we must call upon our leaders to stand up and do what is right. This time our response must consist of more than regret, sorrow and condolence." The statement ended with what would become Gabby's and my rallying cry: "This can no longer wait."

I returned from China five days after the tragedy. The nation was still in mourning. The once-serene town of Newtown was burying its slaughtered children and adults. On a visit there the Sunday after the rampage, President Obama had met with victims' families and held a vigil where he promised to use whatever power he had to prevent shootings like the school massacre.

"What choice do we have?" the president asked. "Are we really prepared to say that we're powerless in the face of such carnage, that the politics are too hard? Are we prepared to say that such violence visited on our children year after year is somehow the price of our freedom?"

Gabby shook her head.

"Surely we can do better than this," he said. "We have an obligation to try."

Gabby and I had been feeling the tug of that same obligation. Sometimes it takes a punch in the face to spring into action. The National Rifle Association landed that punch.

In the days immediately following the Newtown massacre, the NRA was nowhere to be seen or heard from. Our entire nation went into mourning for these families, for this town—for the horror of living in a place where so many young lives could be taken in such a brutal manner.

The NRA remained silent for an entire week. And then Wayne LaPierre, its CEO and executive vice president, took to the microphone at a press conference in Washington, DC, to deliver his organization's response to the tragedy. He immediately derided gun-free school zones, which he claimed made our children targets.

"The truth is that our society is populated by an unknown number of genuine monsters," he said. "People so deranged, so evil, so possessed by voices and driven by demons that no sane person can possibly ever comprehend them. They walk among us every day."

Gabby and I watched the speech from our home in Tucson. We saw LaPierre's eyes getting wider behind his frameless glasses. We listened in growing shock as he blamed the Newtown rampage on the media, on video games, and on weak federal gun prosecutions. Gabby looked at me and pursed her lips. Like the rest of the country, we were taken aback by LaPierre's language, by his insensitivity to the tragedy, and by what seemed like his fringe views. Couldn't the NRA have done better than this unhinged-sounding extremist?

"Add another hurricane, terrorist attack, or some other natural or man-made disaster," LaPierre said, his voice rising, "and you've got a recipe for a national nightmare of violence and victimization."

Hurricanes? Victimization? What about addressing the fact that lethal weapons were in the hands of a young man with a history of severe mental health problems? Not a word about it. Gabby and I—and probably most other Americans listening that day—couldn't believe our ears. What a mess! Surely the NRA would quickly dial back its spokesman's thoughtlessly blurted-out tirade.

Little did we realize at the time that LaPierre's whole performance had been perfectly calculated—and perfectly in line with what the NRA had been saying for years.

LaPierre closed his remarks as aggressively as he began them: "I call on Congress today to act immediately to appropriate whatever is necessary to put armed police officers in every school—and do it now, to make sure that blanket of safety is in place when our children return to school in January."

After the speech, Gabby gazed at me, narrowing her eyes. "Nonsense," she said. "Crazy talk." Then she raised her eyebrows. The message of this gesture was clear: we had to quit *talking*. LaPierre had pushed us over the edge. The NRA's automatic response to every massacre was "more guns," but Gabby and I had faith that Americans were smarter than that.

We couldn't wait any longer. We had to stop talking and start *doing*, with no more delays. Listening to LaPierre's rant, I understood the urgency of convening a national—and, for a change, rational—conversation on the topic of gun violence. *Somebody* had to step up and change the tone of this debate: instead of the usual screeching rhetoric (on both sides), citizens from all over the political spectrum finally seemed ready for a genuine discussion of our shared values and beliefs about guns. Maybe if we could really get talking, we could start agreeing on some straightforward measures to make our country safer.

Gabby and I decided that it was time—long past time—to create an organization that could cut through the NRA's rhetoric and convene a fair-minded dialogue about preventing gun violence. We made a commitment to each other to see this through. But what form would our advocacy take?

* * *

We spent the holidays talking with trusted aides and friends about how we could make the biggest difference. "Maybe we should just take a direct political approach," I suggested. "We could back candidates that agree with us—and with most Americans—on this issue."

Our advisers kept stressing over and over how unusual it was to have two committed gun owners at the helm of this debate. Maybe Gabby and I were in a unique position to promote a pro-gun point of view while emphasizing the importance of putting sensible laws into place. We could work with people from all over the spectrum—cops and veterans, liberals and conservatives, doctors and moms and yes, even NRA members—who supported implementing some basic gun laws. We could give them a forum.

Gabby and I decided to home in on the commonsense issues that the overwhelming majority of Americans—*even* the majority of NRA members—agreed needed to change:

- Expanding background checks and closing loopholes on gun-show and Internet sales
- Strengthening our mental health–reporting system so that people with a history of serious mental health problems are barred from buying firearms
- Aiding women who seek protective orders and barring all abusive partners from gun ownership

20

- Fighting illegal gun trafficking by giving law enforcement better tools and increasing penalties
- Establishing responsible boundaries for high-capacity magazines and the lethality of civilian weaponry

What we considered the centerpiece of our policy push—expanding background checks to all gun sales—wasn't even controversial: a poll released in early 2013, just as we were forming our organization, showed that *nine out of ten* Americans supported the need for stronger background checks.

But turning the will of the people into law isn't as straightforward as it should be. How would we go about fighting for these changes? And how would our group differ from established organizations advocating for more sensible gun laws?

The Brady Campaign to Prevent Gun Violence—named after Jim Brady, President Ronald Reagan's press secretary who was shot in the head in 1981 during an attempt to assassinate Reagan—had helped push through the federal background-check law in 1993 and organize the Million Mom March against gun violence. Gabby and I knew we would work with the Brady Campaign, but we also wanted to venture into elective politics. Another force on the landscape was Mayors Against Illegal Guns, a group founded in 2006 by New York Mayor Michael Bloomberg that represented nine hundred mayors from big cities and small towns across America.

While these and other groups out there were working hard to reform gun laws, no one was representing the interests of reasonable, law-abiding gun owners. It occurred to Gabby and me, as we surveyed the landscape, that the two of us were in a unique position to reform gun laws, moderate the debate in Congress, and make the country safer and saner. As a former Republican, Gabby could see beyond the partisan divide on many issues, including this one. With our centrist positions, our experience, and our visibility—not to mention our patriotism and our own responsible gun ownership—we could build a movement and maneuver the halls of Congress. In electoral politics, we could support our allies while helping defeat those who went against the will of their constituents.

We could teach Americans that you can have it both ways: it is possible to protect the Second Amendment *and* keep our country safer from gun violence.

"Bring balance," Gabby liked to say.

We examined polling data. We searched for allies. We established our goals.

* * *

Gabby and I knew we would face personal challenges. We wanted to make sure we fully understood what we were getting into.

Gabby was an old hand at politicking and advocacy, but she still had trouble articulating her thoughts. She could write, and she could join every discussion and every conference call, but she had a hard time speaking. Better by the week? Yes. Still struggling? Yes. She talked in short bursts. Would the demands of building an organization and being asked to speak in front of groups wear on Gabby and prove too demanding?

"No," she said one day over breakfast in our Tucson breakfast nook. "Let's go."

What about my own dual role, voicing Gabby's thoughts as well as my own? Was I prepared to go before the public on a political matter? As a space shuttle commander, I had done my share of media appearances. You wear many hats as an astronaut, and one of them is becoming a spokesperson. But fielding questions about docking the space shuttle with the space station isn't in the same league as wading into a fierce debate on gun laws. I would be vulnerable in new ways. I'd never worked directly in politics before—would I be able to handle partisan attacks? I would have to learn to be more careful in choosing my words, to say the least. But if Gabby could manage, so could I.

From the start, Gabby and I could see that her advocacy would become intertwined with her recovery. The challenges of creating and building an organization would push her to connect words to thoughts and re-create pathways in her mind. She craved the opportunity to devote herself to this cause. Gabby Giffords was in motion.

Sometimes you just jump right in.

* * *

We knew we would have to leap back into the fundraising realm right away. We would be starting from scratch against the NRA, an organization with more than a century's head start, more than four million members, and an annual budget of $220 million. Waging a big political battle costs big money.

Gabby and I spent hours on conference calls with trusted aides, many of whom had been with Gabby in Congress. Pia Carusone, Gabby's longtime chief of staff, was on the phone with us every day. Pia had been a stalwart presence in the wake of the Tucson shooting and remained close to us even after Gabby stepped down from her seat. Pia was crucial in our embryonic discussions and the creation of our organization. After helping close down Gabby's congressional operation, Pia had taken an important job as chief spokeswoman for Janet Napolitano at the Department of Homeland Security.

"You have to quit your job," I told her. "We're not going to do this unless you become executive director."

* * *

My first fundraising call was to Steve Mostyn, a Texas trial lawyer. We had become friends with Steve and his wife, Amber, while I was an astronaut living in Houston. When Gabby was shot and being treated at a Houston rehabilitation hospital, Steve and Amber had insisted that her parents stay at their home.

The Mostyns were more than personally generous. Steve had contributed millions to local and national candidates, and he was known as a ballsy guy in Texas political circles. When Texas governor Rick Perry refused to debate his opponents in his 2010 reelection race, Mostyn chided him with a full-page ad in twenty-six newspapers with his photo stamped with the headline COWARD.

I phoned Steve a few nights before Christmas. "Steve, we have to do something about this epidemic of gun violence in this country," I said. "Gabby and I want to start an organization to try and get some reasonable legislation passed."

After a long pause, Steve spoke. "Lemme tell you," he said in his Texas drawl, "I own thirty-five guns. You know I like to shoot. Last week I went to a local gun store near my house and bought three thousand rounds of ammunition."

Half were for his 9mm pistols; half were .45 caliber.

He told me how the store clerk helped him load the boxes into his truck before turning to Steve and asking, "Are you going to start a war or something?" Steve responded, "Of course not," and gave him a puzzled look.

"So," I asked, "why did you buy all the ammunition?"

"Because it was on sale and I could," he said.

The same month, Steve told me, he sold an old rusted Jet Ski trailer for $200. The buyer showed up, hooked the trailer to his truck, and drove away. A few days later, the man asked Mostyn to meet him at a local DMV so they could fill out some paperwork necessary to transfer ownership of the trailer.

"So I had to go downtown and take the time to fill out a bunch of forms about an old trailer," he said. "You know how much paperwork I had to do to buy three thousand rounds of ammo? Nothing." He paid cash and didn't even leave his name.

"And we wonder why the murder rate in our country is twenty times what it is in other countries," he said. And then, to my total shock, he added, "Okay—I'll give you a million dollars."

I was blown away—I hadn't expected my first call to produce such a result. Obviously, our organization had struck a nerve with law-abiding gun owners.

Encouraged by Steve's generosity, I made a few more calls that night. Each one was a success. We were a long way from the tens of millions we figured we would need to get in the game in the 2014 election cycle, but it was a darn good start.

Gabby and I had one more gut check, just the two of us, sitting in the shade on the flagstone deck the next afternoon. Nelson settled at her feet. She had fed him and trained him, but that wasn't the only reason he preferred her. We examined the risks of launching our organization.

It could start fast out of the gate and fizzle.

It could starve for lack of money or members.

We might fail to change any minds or laws.

25

The NRA could crush it—and us in the process.

Gabby stopped me. She had been reading about some NRA members, "gun guys" who felt the NRA didn't represent their views. These guys owned guns so they could go hunting on the weekends, or they kept guns in their house for personal protection, but they had no problem with undergoing a basic background check. They'd passed background checks themselves, and they believed every gun owner should do the same. They loved guns, but they were not extremists. Gabby thought the time had come for a group that represented *their* point of view.

After all this discussion, on January 8, 2013—the two-year anniversary of the Tucson massacre—Gabby and I announced the formation of Americans for Responsible Solutions. We hoped it would bring some balance and safety back to our discussions and our laws about gun ownership. We wrote an op-ed for *USA Today* explaining what we wanted to do.

"Special interests purporting to represent gun owners but really advancing the interests of an ideological fringe have used big money and influence to cow Congress into submission," we wrote. "Rather than working to find the balance between our rights and the regulation of a dangerous product, these groups have cast simple protections for our communities as existential threats to individual liberties."

We knew what we were getting into. We would be David against the NRA's Goliath.

If I have learned one thing about Gabby Giffords, it's that she's a fighter, against all odds. This would be a most worthy battle.

CHAPTER TWO

GUN COUNTRY

Tombstone, the iconic Western town, is in the desert of southeast Arizona, thirty miles from the Mexican border.

Tombstone is where Wyatt Earp and his brothers faced down outlaws at the Gunfight at the O.K. Corral, the most famous shoot-out of the frontier era. In 1881, Earp and his brothers Virgil and Morgan traded slugs with a band of bad guys, namely Billy Clanton, Tom McLaury, and his brother Frank. The Earps had brought along their friend, the legendary Doc Holliday, who was wounded in the fusillade. The outlaws fell dead. Wyatt Earp walked away unscathed. It was all over in about thirty seconds.

You can see the bloody battle in the 1957 movie of the same name. Burt Lancaster played Wyatt Earp; Kirk Douglas was Doc Holliday. The same fabled scene was reprised in the 1993 film *Tombstone*, with Val Kilmer and Kurt Russell. A year later Kevin Costner starred in *Wyatt Earp*.

Such movies etched Tombstone in our consciousness as an enchantingly lawless no-man's-land. The Earps are American heroes, and the O.K. Corral has become part of our language, shorthand for the Wild West.

For Gabby and me, Tombstone is a tourist town in the

congressional district Gabby represented. We would take I-10 south and east through Benson, past the Coronado National Forest. Route 80 would take us through the small town of St. David down to Tombstone to visit constituents and check out a road project Gabby had helped fund.

The town is well preserved, even though only a few of its original 110 saloons still line Fremont Street. The brothels are gone, and the silver mines that fueled the town's growth have long since closed down. Tourists come now to sense the frontier, shop, and visit the Boothill Graveyard. Every afternoon, a band of actors in full western regalia reenacts the famous gunfight. The Earps win; the horse rustlers lose. Stores on Main Street sell ten-gallon hats and leather vests and plastic six-shooters in all sizes.

But Tombstone is more than a tourist destination and movie setting. What happened in Tombstone—or how it happened—sheds some light on our feelings about guns as they relate to independence and manhood. Tombstone embodies a particular myth of the Old West that goes something like this: way back on the old frontier, men were men, and as such they settled their fights with guns. Cowboys walked around with a six-shooter strapped to their belts, and shoot-outs were as accepted as cattle drives. Men protected their honor and their women with Colt .45s—and the good guys always prevailed. The gun was holstered to the American sense of rugged individualism.

The problem with that myth is that it's just that: a myth, only half true and very misleading.

* * *

Here's the real story: the Gunfight at the O.K. Corral wasn't about men strutting around brandishing Colt .45s to settle their differences over horses. It was all about Tombstone's gun laws.

In the years before the legendary gun battle, the Tombstone city council had passed Ordinance No. 9, "To Provide Against the Carrying of Deadly Weapons": "It is hereby declared unlawful to carry in the hand or upon the person or otherwise any deadly weapon within the limits of said city of Tombstone, without first obtaining a permit in writing."

Like many towns on the American frontier, Tombstone wanted to grow by attracting new businesses and transplants. True, men and women out on the range needed guns to protect themselves from bears and mountain lions, to kill dinner, to defend their outposts. But in cities and towns in the early West, laws and regulations mandated that cowboys check their guns at the city line. Many towns passed regulations that forced men to leave their guns at the livery, where they would get a metal token to redeem their weapons when they left town.

All those westerns depicting grizzled men in saloons wearing holsters with the Colt .45s they used to settle disputes over poker have little bearing on history. Cowboys had to disarm before they bellied up to the bar.

Even infamous Dodge City had a big billboard in the middle of town that read: THE CARRYING OF FIREARMS STRICTLY PROHIBITED. Dodge City recorded just five killings by gunfire in 1878, its most homicidal year. Many states outlawed carrying concealed weapons in the 1800s. By 1859 Kentucky, Louisiana, Indiana, Tennessee, Virginia, Alabama, and Ohio had banned concealed carry in public. Montana followed in 1887. Three years later, Oklahoma passed a law to make it illegal to carry a concealed weapon not only in towns and cities but across the entire territory.

But in Tombstone, the outlaws ignored the town ordinance and continued to walk around with concealed weapons. The Earps and Doc Holliday were trying to enforce the law by disarming them. The gunfight that day was the result of their disagreement. The Earps faced down the bad guys because they refused to turn in their weapons, as the law ordered.

Billy Clanton's brother Ike had already been arrested and fined for walking around Tombstone armed. Ike and his band of rustlers were still wearing guns strapped to their sides when the Earps and Doc Holliday confronted them.

"Throw up your hands," Virgil Earp ordered the gang, according to his court testimony. "I have come to disarm you."

The bad guys had broken a gun law, and they paid with their lives.

*　*　*

Gabby was born and raised a little over an hour from Tombstone, though Arizona had changed a great deal in the century since the infamous showdown that took place there. Growing up in the suburban Tucson neighborhood of Tanque Verde, north and east of the city, Gabby rode horses, sang in school plays, occasionally sneaked out of the house at night to meet a boyfriend, and studied hard and got good grades.

Her father, Spencer, was a businessman. He took over El Campo Tires from his father and grew it into a regional enterprise. Gabby's mother, Gloria, was an artist with an unconventional streak. Sometimes, when she showed up at school to pick up Gabby and her older sister, Melissa, Gloria might be dressed in costume, just to lighten up the day for her daughters and mortify them in front of their friends—a surefire tactic for toughening them up. It was a good early lesson for Gabby about not worrying too much about what people thought of her. Gloria was active in the local art community. Spencer served on the Tucson school board. He tried to make it home every night for dinner to trade news of the day and discuss politics or art or whatever came up.

The Giffords family hiked and camped and drove across the Mexican border to explore almost every summer. Spencer and Gloria would drop Gabby and Melissa off at a Mexican summer camp, where they learned Spanish from native speakers and met kids from a different culture. Over the course of those summers, the girls got an education about life beyond the suburbs. They learned to open their hearts to people from other cultures or less fortunate circumstances than theirs.

Melissa, Gabby's older sister by two years, saw how those trips fed Gabby's innate drive to give back and help others. No one who knew Gabby well back then was surprised that she would devote her life to public service.

Gabby loved horses, and her parents encouraged her horsemanship. She mucked out stalls to help buy her first horse, Dink. She took her second horse, Buckstretcher, with her to college. It gave her a meaningful life experience that she liked to talk about on the campaign trail: "I learned a lot cleaning out those stalls. It was good training, all of that manure shoveling, for when I entered politics."

* * *

Few of us think of the modern West as all that wild. Isn't it strange, then, that the Clantons could legally wear holsters with revolvers in Tombstone today? In fact, they could walk the streets of Tombstone with a Glock semiautomatic pistol

31

ENOUGH

tucked into their belts, under their coats. Neither the Earps
nor the local sheriff could lawfully demand that they drop
their weapons.

Arizona has some of the most liberal gun laws in the
nation. It is one of only four states that allows residents aged
twenty-one or over to carry concealed weapons, without any
training, though more states are considering such laws. Any
adult over eighteen can carry a loaded weapon openly, without a permit.

Gabby entered politics with a respect for long rifles and
holstered guns. Under Arizona law, she could have carried
a pistol in her purse or on her belt all the way to the statehouse, or down Fremont Street in Tombstone.

When Gabby announced her first run for the state legislature in 2000, she was well aware that guns were as plentiful
as cacti in her state, that many children grew up in homes
where shooting guns was routine, and that the majority of
her colleagues in the Phoenix statehouse were bent on loos-
ening laws on gun ownership.

During her terms in the state legislature and Senate, and
when she ran for Congress in 2006, Gabby supported gun
rights. Her opponent in that first campaign, Randy Graf,
was a far-right conservative. As a state representative, he had
introduced a bill that would have allowed Arizonans to carry
guns into bars and restaurants. (This measure later passed—
but only after Graf added a provision stating that patrons
with weapons cannot drink alcohol.) But gun rights were
by no means a centerpiece of the campaign. During that first
race for Congress and the succeeding ones, Gabby turned
the debate toward immigration and education, health care,
the wars in Iraq and Afghanistan, and solar energy.

When gun rights came up, she would often say: "I follow

32

the lead of law enforcement. The mentally ill and convicted felons shouldn't have access to firearms."

Apparently, that stance wasn't good enough for the National Rifle Association. While the NRA supported Gabby's opponents in her three congressional races, it didn't devote serious resources to defeating her. During her congressional terms, the NRA gave Gabby a C rating. The group saw her as neither a strong ally nor a foe. She occupied the rational middle.

Gun legislation did not factor into Gabby's state or congressional campaigns. She won elections by walking door to door, by raising plenty of cash, by stressing her record of fighting for issues that mattered to her constituents: immigration reform, improved public education, and protecting the environment.

In her victory speech for her first congressional race she said: "I'm ready to roll up my sleeves to get to work for the children in our country, who deserve the best schools, the best education."

Gabby won as a woman of the West who could connect with Arizonans. Gun rights were never a major issue.

When the Supreme Court in 2008 struck down the District of Columbia's ban on handguns and affirmed an individual's right to bear arms in the Heller decision, Gabby agreed. "As a gun owner," she said, "I am a strong supporter of the Second Amendment." She had joined the amicus brief supporting the lower-court ruling that struck down the DC ban leading up to the Supreme Court ruling. "This is a commonsense decision that reaffirms the Constitutional right— and Arizona tradition—of owning firearms."

Gabby later voted to repeal DC's handgun ban. "We have a long tradition of gun ownership in the United States," she said. "It is a tradition which every law-abiding citizen should be able to enjoy."

In her last race for Congress, Gabby ran against Jesse Kelly, no relation, perhaps her most conservative opponent. With the support of the Tea Party, Kelly ran hard against Gabby as an ally of President Obama. Though the race was close and one of the last in the country to be called that election, Gabby prevailed. Again, gun rights were not a major factor. Her constituents trusted her on numerous other issues that were important to them.

*　　*　　*

Some dads haul around briefcases stuffed with legal briefs. My father took a .25 Colt handgun with him to work. The gun was a tool of his trade. It might have been the smallest-caliber weapon he was permitted to carry. Richard Kelly was a detective in West Orange, New Jersey, and when he wasn't at work, he kept his gun in the kitchen cabinet.

My mother, Patricia, had law enforcement in her family. Her sister was an FBI agent; her brother was a cop. She started working as a secretary but she became a cop, too, the first female police officer in West Orange. She served on patrol, and back in the 1970s her service weapon was a .38 revolver.

My twin brother, Scott, and I grew up in a working-class home where firearms were an accepted part of life. Scott and I were rowdy kids. We fought with each other and our neighbors. We had our run-ins with the local cops, who let us off but made sure our parents knew what we were up to. None of our childhood neighbors in New Jersey would ever have predicted that *both* Scott and I would grow up to be astronauts—the only twins or even siblings ever to have flown in space (though never at the same time!).

When I was a troublemaking kid, I would sometimes take my dad's pistol out of the kitchen cabinet and show it off to friends. Luckily, he never caught me. My brother and I were raised with a healthy respect for guns and the damage they could do.

When I was in tenth grade, my mother was dispatched to a home where a young man had killed his parents. He was holding his sister hostage. When she arrived on the scene at three A.M., the guy was shooting out the window. My mom dove for cover. Unfortunately, she landed on a pile of dog crap. If she lifted her head, she was a target; if she kept it down, she wanted to puke. Reinforcements finally arrived, and the man surrendered, but it was no joke to me that my mother spent the night getting shot at. This was my mom's one and only experience of bullets flying at her in her entire career.

Guns were part of our lives. We were comfortable with them and would soon have them in our work, too.

*   *   *

Turns out I was a pretty decent shot.

At the US Merchant Marine Academy I was trained with a Mark 1 rifle as part of my education toward a direct commission into the United States Navy. This M1 Garand was practically a relic. It was the weapon of choice during World War II, but now it had a home as the qualification rifle for cadets and midshipmen. I qualified as a sharpshooter.

In Navy flight school, we never picked up a gun. The demands of learning to fly a fighter jet and operate a weapons system were so time-consuming that we never even discussed small-arms training. If we wanted to be proficient with a sidearm, we'd have to figure out that part on our own time. Some of us did. While training in Beeville, Texas, my flight-school buddies and I would often head out to a remote part of an outlying air base, where we would do some bird hunting and target shooting with pistols. We'd set up cans and bottles and challenge each other to see who was the best shot. I might not have been the best, but I could hold my own.

When I graduated from flight school in December of 1987, my dad bought me a 9mm handgun. He had served in the Army as a paratrooper in the Eighty-second Airborne Division and understood the value of a decent weapon.

"You might need this one day," he said.

The day came sooner than I thought.

In the summer of 1990, Saddam Hussein's Iraqi army invaded Kuwait, beginning the Gulf War. I was stationed in Japan aboard the aircraft carrier USS *Midway*. I went to war piloting an A-6E Intruder, an all-weather ground-attack jet and medium-range bomber that could carry a lot of ordnance. It was the workhorse of naval aviation. The F-14 Tomcat is often the airplane that comes to mind when most folks think about naval aircraft, because it starred in the movie *Top Gun*. As we flew A-6E missions into Iraq, the Tomcat pilots flew circles over the battle group, protecting the ships from enemy fighters that rarely came. But the A-6E Intruder was the airplane that put the bombs on target to punish and destroy the enemy.

I took the 9mm with me to Japan and stowed it on base at the armory while we were in port. Japanese law prohibited people from keeping a handgun in their home, and I lived off base in a Japanese house. As we got closer to deployment, I took comfort knowing my dad's present would accompany me. Many of the other pilots were not so fortunate. They had to settle for the Navy's five-shooter revolvers stored in the ship's armory. A month prior to going into combat, these guns were delivered to our ready room to strap on and defend our-selves in case we got shot down. We all got a big laugh. They were rusted—and who had even heard of a five-shooter? It seemed as if the Pentagon had tried to save a buck by only contracting for five holes in the cylinder instead of six.

All of a sudden, pilots were sending frantic letters back home: "Buy me a gun, and send it quick!" One received a huge package that contained an oversize handgun with a large magazine and long barrel. It was an Israeli Military Industries Desert Eagle. I think it was of the .44 caliber variety. Word got around the squadron. Gun envy broke out. Skipper Terry Toms brought us all together for a chat in the ready room.

Terry Toms was the leader that I tried most to emulate in my twenty-five-year Navy career. He was tough but under-standing and cared about his troops and the pilots and bom-bardier-navigators. He was one of the few pilots in our air wing who had any combat experience, having served at the tail end of the Vietnam War. He could also be a common-sense kind of guy.

"Let me give you some advice," Skipper Toms told us. "If you don't want to fly with the Navy-issued five-shooter, I understand. But don't get a gun so big that you won't mind having the Iraqis shove it up your ass when you're shot down and captured. Because if you think you're fighting your way out of a bad situation, you're kidding yourselves."

Even back in 1990, Skipper Toms understood the chal-lenges of the "good guy" with a gun.

*   *   *

When I flew across the Persian Gulf straight into Iraqi air defenses, I carried the 9mm under my left arm, but it didn't help me survive thirty-nine combat missions.

Winston Churchill famously said: "There is nothing more exhilarating than being shot at with no result."

Well, I think that the yahoos who go on and on about how everyone should be armed so good guys can defend against bad guys have no clue. They have never felt the fear and adrenaline rush of combat. Most have no idea how that feels. Try to keep your head on straight when bullets or missiles are whizzing by. It's not like *Dirty Harry*. Or, in my case, *Top Gun*.

On one of my early missions over the Persian Gulf, I flew off the *Midway* in my A-6 and headed toward the coast with Paul Fujimura, my bombardier-navigator. We spotted two Iraqi ships steaming toward Iran. After a closer look we determined they were Polnocny amphibious assault ships that the Iraqis had purchased from Russia or the Soviet Union. We radioed back to the battle group for orders—sink 'em or let them find safe haven in Iran. We were loaded with a single five-hundred-pound laser-guided bomb and two MK-20 Rockeye cluster bombs, designed to take out armored vehicles and troops. If placed correctly, they might work on a ship as well.

We got orders to attack, so we set up for the release of the laser-guided bomb. Due to some rotten luck and a little bit of bad flying on my part, the bomb hit the water just behind the ship. It was the first and only miss for Paul and me during the war.

The Iraqis immediately opened up on us with their anti-aircraft gun. It was daytime, so we didn't see the tracers, but we could see the puffs of smoke at the exit of the barrels of the gun. We maneuvered wildly, jinking left and right to make ourselves a very difficult target.

As I wrenched the plane around, up and down, I told Paul to set me up for a visual delivery of the two remaining bombs—our Rockeye cluster munitions. I pulled the airplane over into a 20-degree dive from about six thousand feet. In order to get a weapon accurately on target, at some point you have to just suck it up and stop moving all over the sky, thus presenting yourself as a stable target to the enemy. I steadied the airplane to deliver the payload. Bullets whizzed by our cockpit. We dove at the ship. The targeting computer provided me with a constant impact point for the weapons. As the bombsight symbol on the heads-up display crossed over the ship, I pickled off the two bombs and immediately started jinking again: right, left, down, up, and as unpredictably as possible. The Iraqi guns were still firing as the Rockeyes exploded across the back half of one of the Iraqi ships. One gun fell silent. The gun on the second ship continued to fire as we beat feet back to the *Midway*.

At that moment, I could relate to Churchill's exhilaration. To be in combat, to see, hear, and feel enemy rounds, is unlike any other human experience. Even after preparing for live combat for years, I couldn't have known what the controlled chaos would be like in reality.

Paul and I flew thirty-nine combat missions over Iraq and Kuwait. We attacked buildings and tanks and missile batteries and trucks and troops. For me the hardest part was attacking troops in the open with cluster munitions. While we understood that the most basic tenet of war is to kill the enemy, that part wasn't fun. A good soldier possesses some form of mutual respect for the enemy on the battlefield, and while we never hesitated killing him, we never took our orders lightly.

We tried to handle the deadly weapons of war with the utmost respect.

* * *

Gabby and I believe the Tombstone city fathers had a similar respect for guns. They passed laws to regulate these deadly weapons in town because the American West was awash with guns, and they respected their lethality.

When Americans ventured into the frontier during the nineteenth century and settled the open spaces west of the Mississippi River all the way to the Pacific Ocean, they packed guns—often Colt .45s—along with their horses and plows. Samuel Colt was a genius at marketing his new "revolver," a pistol with a rotating cylinder that could hold many bullets and fire them with a repeated pull of the trigger.

"God created men," said one of Colt's ads. "Colonel Colt made them equal."

For the next century, guns were as common as furniture in American households, especially in farm country and the open spaces of the South, Midwest, and West. We kept them around mostly to hunt, sometimes for self-defense, often because they were handed down from generation to generation.

Over time, guns have become less prevalent and less relevant, especially in the last forty years. Fewer of us own guns. As more and more of us have migrated into urban areas, fewer of us hunt for our livelihoods. The crime rate in this country has plummeted dramatically over the last thirty years, for reasons experts are still struggling to understand. The need to be armed, so intense even a century ago, has diminished.

Gabby and I were initially surprised by a recent national report that showed just how drastically gun ownership has declined over the last four decades. The General Social Survey is a public-opinion survey conducted by the University of Chicago every two years to assess Americans' attitudes and feelings on a variety of issues. In the early 1970s, survey respondents' gun-ownership rate was about 50 percent. That number dropped in the next two decades, according to the survey, and by 2012 it had fallen to 34 percent.

Gallup polls have shown a similar decline. Its surveys found that more than 50 percent of Americans said they had a gun in their house in the 1990s, but that number fell to the mid-40s over the next fifteen years, representing "a clear societal change."

But what exactly propelled that change?

Gabby and I figured it must be because Americans have been moving from the country to the city. City dwellers, we assumed, have less reason to hunt and keep guns around. But the study showed that gun ownership has fallen in all regions of our country. Fewer Americans in cities, towns, suburbs, *and* rural areas own guns. Most surprisingly, the rate has fallen in the South and the West.

Hunting as an American tradition seems to be waning. No question. Whether it's for white-tailed deer, bear, or "varmints," as Mitt Romney was fond of saying on the campaign trail—or, as is the case here in southern Arizona, mountain lion—we just aren't hunting as much as we were fifty years ago. The University of Chicago study found that only 20 percent of US men in 2012 said they hunted; in 1977 that number was around 36 percent. As our country gets more urbanized, kids are more likely to be spending their weekends shooting basketballs than rifles.

Also, in cities and suburbs from coast to coast, there's been a steep drop in violent crime. Last year the US was on track for the lowest homicide rate in a century. To the surprise of law-enforcement agencies, major crimes continued to drop even during the recession. So perhaps across the board people feel less threatened. Fewer believe they need a gun in their home for self-protection.

What, then, explains the fact that there are still an estimated three hundred million guns—roughly the same number as there are people in this country—in American homes? And how are we to understand reports that gun sales skyrocketed after the Newtown shooting rampage? Sturm, Ruger & Co., the fourth-largest firearms maker in the country, reported an increase in sales in the first nine months of 2013 of 44 percent over two years earlier, perhaps as a result of the NRA's warnings that restrictions on gun buying were about to get more serious.

The simplest answer is that fewer Americans own more guns—many, many more guns (and more ammunition, too). Some gun owners might have one or two hunting rifles in their safe; others might have a small arsenal of thirty weapons. A study based on the 2004 National Firearms Survey found that 20 percent of America's gun owners own 65 percent of the guns in this country. And *these* are the people the NRA is addressing when their leaders talk about a vast "confiscation scheme" of guns and the eventual "total disarmament of freedom-loving people all over the world."

Survivalists, like the kind Gabby and I occasionally watch on *Doomsday Preppers*, are becoming an increasingly common part of our landscape. There are people in this country who are susceptible to extreme beliefs, and some of these people stockpile guns, especially when the NRA preys on their fears.

Gabby and I have also come to believe that the concentration of many guns in the possession of fewer Americans has contributed to the hardened stance of some gun owners. And to hear the NRA tell it, even the hint of a restriction—

even perfectly reasonable ones, like requiring background checks for gun purchases and putting an end to illegal Internet sales—is a gross infringement on their rights.

We understand that argument. But we do live in a democracy, where we try to adhere to laws that protect the welfare of all citizens.

Just as Tombstone town leaders passed laws in 1879 to keep six-guns off the streets for the welfare of all, we need to draft laws to keep guns in the hands of law-abiding citizens and away from those who would do us harm.

In the spring of 2006, Gabby drove down to Tombstone to march in the Rose Parade, the centerpiece of the town's annual Rose Tree Festival. It's a commemoration of the town's softer side. In 1885, a cutting from a rose tree arrived from Scotland as a gift for a homesick bride. The cutting has grown into one of the world's largest rosebushes. The day begins with a pancake breakfast and builds toward the parade of covered wagons—and "the Earp brothers," of course.

After the parade, Gabby was shaking hands and taking pictures with folks in full western regalia. A fellow stopped her and asked: "Where do you stand on the Second Amendment?"

"I stand firmly behind it," she said. "And I own a Glock."

Gabby had a Glock 17 9mm semiautomatic pistol, a reliable and easy-to-handle weapon. The Glock is all about point and shoot. The only safety is a small lever on the trigger that must be depressed before the trigger can be pulled. If you are not pulling the trigger, the gun shouldn't fire. It was the perfect gun for Gabby to protect herself in her Tucson neighborhood.

Meanwhile, Gabby's parents, Gloria and Spencer, had moved to a house they had built deep in the hills southeast of Tucson, miles down a gravel road. It was the terrain of critters, rattlesnakes, and mountain lions. On our visits we would occasionally bring our guns and get some target practice.

After Gabby and I married in November 2007, I bought Gloria a .357 Smith & Wesson revolver for her protection. Probably not the smartest gift for just any mother-in-law, but Gloria and I get along well.

During the 2010 health care debate, I was nervous about what was going on in Gabby's congressional district. As always, Gabby wanted to hear from her constituents, and she held town-hall meetings in Tucson and around her district. Opposition to President Obama's health care reforms was intense across the country, but anger boiled over in Gabby's district. At one meeting in Douglas, a man came to protest Gabby's vote with a gun in his shoulder harness. He was silent and respectful, but at one point he leaned down and the gun fell out and crashed to the floor.

"When you represent a district that includes the home of the O.K. Corral and Tombstone, 'the town too tough to die,' nothing's a surprise in Cochise County," Gabby told the *Arizona Republic*.

On Sunday, March 21, 2010, Gabby voted in the majority to pass Obama's Affordable Care Act. Gabby had watched the e-mails, slurs, and rhetoric become "incredibly heated." Tea Party activists had used the corner by her office as a gathering point for their protests. Her staffers arrived at their district office Monday morning after the vote to find plywood covering the glass door because someone had smashed it out, perhaps by bullet or brick.

"Are you afraid?" NBC reporter Chuck Todd asked Gabby that morning the news broke. "Are you fearful today?"

"You know," she said, "I'm not." After describing some of the heated rhetoric, she went on, "Our democracy is a light—a beacon really—around the world because we effect change at the ballot box and not because of these outbursts of violence."

But as Gabby would learn, gun country is no longer just a dusty ghost town in the Arizona desert. Gun country is everywhere these days: a basement in suburban Maryland, a rural church in Georgia, a supermarket parking lot in suburban Tucson.

The American West might've been wild, but it wasn't lawless. Modern-day America is a different story. It seems like you can bring guns anywhere you want, even if you're a criminal or have a dangerous mental illness. And that's got to change.

CHAPTER THREE

ACTIVE SHOOTER
IN TUCSON

On the morning of Saturday, January 8, 2011, Gabby phoned me from Tucson. "I'm on my way to a Congress on Your Corner," she said. "I'll call you when it's over."

We took comfort in starting the day with each other. We tried to talk every morning and every night, and our inboxes would ping with little updates throughout the day, especially when we weren't in the same city. That morning Gabby was on her way to a Safeway supermarket on the northwest side of Tucson to visit with constituents for her first town-hall meeting of the new congressional session. I was in Houston.

"Okay, sweetie," I answered.

"I love you," she said.

"Love you, too," I responded.

The first week of 2011 had already been tumultuous. Gabby was starting her third term in Congress after a tough reelection campaign. More than three hundred people had jammed into her congressional office for an open house before her swearing-in. My parents, Richard and Patricia, were there, along with Gloria and Spencer. Gabby shined in those moments. She's always reminded me of Bill Clinton in her gift for connecting with people. Everyone got a hug.

I was training to command my final space shuttle mission. I was also contemplating my future. Always the raging optimist, Gabby wanted me to stick with the Navy and restart my career in the military after fifteen years at NASA. She thought that with some hard work, I could get promoted to admiral and could continue my service. I wasn't so sure. My twin brother, Scott, would be staying on at NASA, but I had no clear sense of the direction my own future would take.

We were also in the midst of trying to have a baby through IVF. Gabby was scheduled to have a crucial medical procedure at the Bethesda Naval Hospital on Monday, January 10. We were hoping she would be pregnant within the next few months.

On the second day of the new Congress on January 6, representatives gave a reading of the Constitution on the House floor. Gabby had originally been scheduled to read the Second Amendment, and as a strong supporter of the right to bear arms, that would have been an honor. But as a favor to a Republican colleague, the GOP leadership in the House changed the lineup at the last moment and Gabby got to read the First Amendment, her favorite.

"Congress shall make no law," she declared, "respecting an establishment of religion, or prohibiting the free exercise thereof; or abridging the freedom of speech, or of the press; or the right of the people peaceably to assemble, and to petition the Government for a redress of grievances."

The next night, a Friday, Gabby flew home to Arizona. While she was in the air, we both received an e-mail from Kevin Bleyer, a writer for Jon Stewart's *Daily Show* and a close friend. Stewart had made fun of Arizona more than a dozen times in 2010 for its more extreme political moments and politicians. Bleyer sent a link about a state representative, Steve Farley, who said his goal for 2011 was to keep Arizona off Stewart's show. I was amused.

"My poor state," Gabby wrote to Kevin and me. "The nut jobs have stolen it away from the good people of Arizona." The next day Gabby planned to spend time with some of those good people.

* * *

Gabby loved to visit with her constituents, even when they disagreed with her—as some did often and loudly. She stayed connected to the people in her district through e-mail and phone calls, she met with them at homes and town-hall meetings, but her most reliable and often rewarding face-to-face gatherings took place during her Congress on Your Corner events.

Here's how they worked: Gabby's staff would put out word that Gabby was heading to a certain neighborhood. She wouldn't give a speech. She came simply to hear from her constituents. Some came to ask for help with Social Security or another federal agency. Others sought to change her mind on legislation. More than a few came to show support for her stand on health care or immigration. Sometimes people just wanted to meet Gabby, period. Everyone got about five minutes with the congresswoman. Some events would draw twenty, some two hundred.

No one in her office was surprised when Gabby announced, late that Wednesday night, that she wanted to use the first weekend of her third term for a Congress on Your Corner. Thirty-year-old Gabe Zimmerman, Gabby's director of community outreach in Tucson, said he'd have no problem organizing the event on such short notice. "I can do it in my sleep," he claimed with characteristic good humor.

Gabe and Ron Barber, Gabby's district director, quickly settled on a Safeway parking lot in the northwest Tucson neighborhood of Casas Adobes.

Word went out on her website. Constituents received e-mail alerts. The staff used an automated calling system to reach people in the neighborhood, and Gabby tweeted, "My 1st Congress on Your Corner starts now. Please stop by to let me know what is on your mind or tweet me later."

Gabby put on a red jacket and dark skirt and drove herself the eight miles from downtown to the Safeway. The event was planned for ten A.M. She arrived a few minutes early.

She didn't like to be late.

* * *

We know the grim facts of what transpired in the next fifteen minutes. We lost dear friends and neighbors. We almost lost Gabby. Our lives would never be the same.

But there were some details of that day we could not face at first. It was hard enough comprehending the carnage and mourning the loss of the victims. We spent the following two years focusing on Gabby's health and establishing our new lives in Tucson. Some information Gabby and I learned only very recently.

In the immediate aftermath, Gabby had zero interest in knowing anything about the man we called "the shooter." The events of January 8 were too painful, and the energy we gave to her recovery consumed us. But two years later, when we decided that we would begin a public campaign to address gun violence in our communities, we felt the time was now right to delve deeper into that day. We wanted to understand as much as we could about what happened and, the more difficult question, why. In meetings with prosecutors and in reading nearly three thousand pages of verbatim interviews and investigative findings, the story of the day unfolded.

Here's what we learned—about the shooter, the victims, the heroes, and ourselves.

*   *   *

At about the same time that Gabby and I began that Saturday, January 8, with our regular phone call to check in, a young man in Tucson was on a mission to buy bullets.

Jared Lee Loughner's mother, Amy, hadn't slept well. She got up a few times that previous night, once to take NyQuil. Every time she checked her son's room, his light was on. She figured he was up all night. In fact, her son was not in the house. At 12:29 A.M. that Saturday he had checked into a Motel 6 close to the railroad tracks on Tucson's western edge.

When she arose at eight A.M., she realized her son was gone.

Loughner, just twenty-two years old, had used room 411 in the motel as his base of operations for a number of errands before dawn. At 2:19 A.M. he drove his black 1969 Chevy Nova to a Walgreens to pick up developed photos from film he had dropped off Friday night. About two hours later, he posted a bulletin with one of the photos on MySpace that read: "Goodbye friends. Please don't be mad at me."

Shortly after seven A.M., Loughner drove to the Walmart in the Foothills Mall, walked in the grocery entrance, and asked for the sporting goods department. He had a black beanie on his head, pulled very low over his eyes, and a black hoodie

51

sweatshirt over khaki pants. At the sporting goods counter, Loughner asked for a box of 9mm bullets. He was shifting nervously from side to side. The clerk said there were none in the case.

"Can you check in the back?" he asked.

Loughner unnerved the clerk, who went to the back and returned empty-handed. He didn't even check for the bullets because he didn't feel comfortable selling ammunition to Loughner, who looked unstable and angry. Loughner wheeled around and ran out of the store.

Loughner's friends and family would not have been surprised by the clerk's assessment. The only child of Randy and Amy Loughner, he had seemed to grow more strange and distant over the years. Randy, who worked for a carpet company, and Amy, who managed parks for the Pima County Natural Resources Department, saw their son as an average kid, though a bit of a loner. Their boy changed when he reached Mountain View High School.

At sixteen, Loughner grew tall and thin and wore his hair long. He played drums and saxophone with Tyler Zuern, one of his high school buddies. Loughner smoked a fair amount of pot, but he would also experiment with LSD and psychedelic mushrooms. He told his mother he had tried cocaine. Zuern and Loughner were close for a time, but Loughner always seemed to have trouble relating to people. He came off as smart but troubled. When his girlfriend broke up with him, he talked often about how he was going to commit suicide. Zuern tried to talk him out of it. Loughner would show friends where he had cut himself.

Another friend, Zach Osler, didn't like to spend time at Loughner's house. To Osler, it was a hostile environment. One time Loughner told him: "Hey, I don't want to be at my house. You know, my dad's drunk." In high school, Loughner's friends recall him, too, getting drunk enough at one party that he got alcohol poisoning. He dropped out of Mountain View in 2006. Two years later, Loughner tried to enlist in the Army. He admitted to using marijuana and was rejected.

After high school, a few friends would occasionally hang out with Loughner, but they had a hard time maintaining contact. He sent strange text messages. He started posting bizarre videos online, including one in which he burned an American flag. In his "My Final Thoughts" video, text appears on the screen with background music. He goes off on a rant about creating currency based on gold and silver, reels off strings of numbers, and writes: "I define terrorist." His last lines are: "No! I won't trust in God! What's government if words don't have meaning?"

One by one, his friends dropped out of his life. One longtime friend, Bryce Tierney, said he felt his buddy had become "weird, like, in a dark way."

*   *   *

Loughner held down a part-time job as a sales assistant at an Eddie Bauer store for about a year. He was eventually fired. By early 2010 he had been living with his parents for more than a year. He enrolled at Pima Community College for the spring semester, signing up for classes in English, math, and biology.

In the English course, after a classmate read a poem, Loughner spoke up, rambling about abortion, wars, and killing people, asking: "Why don't we just strap bombs to babies?" His English instructor was alarmed enough to notify campus police on February 5. She said Loughner was "creepy" and had a "dark personality." Campus police checked Loughner's records, found some "prior drug involvement," but took no action.

Campus police received four more complaints of Loughner's "suspicious activity" in 2010 from instructors. Math professor Ben McGahee had never had a student quite like Jared Loughner. During class he laughed hysterically to himself while shaking and trembling. After the first few days of class, students said they were scared of him. One day McGahee asked Loughner to pipe down.

"That's the US Constitution," Loughner told his teacher, pointing to the wall, "and you've broken my First Amendment rights." McGahee kicked him out of the course.

On September 23, 2010, Loughner posted a video on YouTube in which he called Pima Community College his "genocide" school. Walking and talking behind his handheld camera, Loughner tours the campus in the dark. "We're examining the torture of students," he says at one point. He talks about mind control and losing his freedom of speech and says: "I am in a terrible place."

Six days later, campus police came to the Loughners' home. Randy Loughner asked them to wait until he put away the dogs before he invited the two officers into the garage. In front of Jared and his parents, they reviewed the reports of Loughner's increasingly bizarre behavior in class. They described the "genocide" school video. They read the college's official letter of expulsion.

Jared Loughner never stopped staring at them. "I realize now this is all a scam," he said.

The letter said Loughner would not be allowed back on campus unless he had a mental health evaluation. The officers advised the Loughners to have their son evaluated. The letter and the two policemen also suggested they remove any guns from the house, because their son might be a danger to himself or others.

Jared Loughner had bought a shotgun the year before at a Sportsman's Warehouse, a national chain with a location near his home. Randy Loughner found his son's shotgun and locked it in the trunk of his own car.

Pima Community College police contacted the US Bureau of Alcohol, Tobacco and Firearms the day Loughner was expelled. The Pima officers asked for any records relating to guns and Jared Lee Loughner.

"I did not come up with any gun info on this guy," an ATF agent replied on October 1. "Let me know if you need anything else."

*　　*　　*

A few days after Christmas, Loughner went to visit two high school buddies, Derek Heintz and Anthony Kuck, who shared an apartment. Heintz was in the kitchen cooking dinner.

"Guess what?" Loughner said. "I got a gun." He pulled a Glock 9mm pistol from his belt.

"What the hell," Heintz said. "Why do you need that?" Heintz thought there was something odd about Loughner's face. He was used to the shaved head. He noticed that Loughner had shaved his eyebrows, too.

"Home protection," Loughner responded.

"There's no need for it here," Heintz said. He didn't know much about guns and didn't ever consider that his friend might own one.

On November 30, 2010, two months after Randy Loughner confiscated his son's shotgun, Loughner had purchased the Glock 19 at Sportsman's Warehouse, the same store where he had bought his shotgun. He paid $559.66 for the handgun, plus a fifteen-round magazine and a box of ammunition.

The Glock 9mm pistol is a matte-black handgun that can fire bullets as fast as you can squeeze the trigger. Police, military, and criminals favor the weapon for its easy handling and reliability. Glock, an Austrian company, entered the US market in 1985 and soon overtook competitors like Smith & Wesson, which had provided .38 caliber revolvers to police for decades. Glock declines to provide sales figures, but more than 65 percent of American police departments now carry the semiautomatic Glocks. In *The Gun Digest Book of the Glock*, Patrick Sweeney says there were more than one million Glocks in the US by 1996. Made of plastic, other synthetics, and metal, Glocks are comparatively light and easy to fire, which makes them popular in the civilian market.

"Can I hold it?" Heintz asked. Loughner's friend took out the magazine and extracted a bullet from the chamber. Heintz wound up keeping one round.

Anthony Kuck was not as amused. He was fed up with Loughner and his rants about currency and the corrupt government and how society was against him. When Loughner showed him the Glock, Kuck asked: "Why the hell do you have this?"

Loughner gave him the line about home protection. Kuck asked him to leave.

* * *

When the two Pima Community College police officers showed up at the Loughners' house and recommended Jared Loughner have a mental health examination, his mother and his father knew their son was not well.

Their son had been out of a job for a year. Amy and Randy

would give him spending cash. They knew Jared's behavior was not normal. He would close the door to his room and conduct full-scale conversations with himself, make odd noises, laugh, gesticulate to someone who was not there. Amy Loughner thought it was odd.

She knew her son had smoked pot and tried other drugs, including cocaine. She and Randy knew he'd had a drinking problem. Amy feared that his behavior was caused by methamphetamines. They tested him for drugs. It came up negative. Jared promised them he had quit drinking.

But was their son angry? His mother knew he was furious with the college for expelling him, and she was aware of his vague antipathy toward the government, but she didn't see him as hate-filled. Randy Loughner saw his son's angry side. Getting fired from Eddie Bauer had put his son in a tailspin. When Pima Community College expelled him, he became distraught. He felt the campus police had harassed him. "Pigs," he called them. Randy Loughner sympathized with his son. He believed Jared was a smart kid who had gotten a raw deal and had become an outcast. The firing and expulsion had altered him in ways his father could not fathom.

"I tried to talk with him," Randy would later tell investigators. "But you can't, he wouldn't let you. Lost, lost, and just didn't want to communicate with me no more."

His parents asked Jared to see a mental health specialist. He refused. They knew he kept journals in a safe in his bedroom. They tried to read their son's writings, but they found the words written in a different language, impossible to decipher.

Investigators were later able to read Jared Loughner's journals. They found an entry as early as December 6, 2010, that said that he had plans to assassinate Gabby. It turns out he had attended a speech she had given at Pima Community

College. In a Q&A after the talk, he had asked her: "What is government if words have no meaning?"

Whatever response Gabby gave to the strange question, Loughner was not impressed.

"Can you believe it," he told his friend Bryce Tierney. "They wouldn't answer my question."

"Dude," Tierney said, "no one's going to answer that."

Loughner came away calling Gabby "a fake" and complained when her name came up, but his buddies never got the sense he hated her. Gabby's staff sent Loughner a letter thanking him for attending the speech. In a box of his writings, investigators found the letter along with notes about his assassination plans. He had written "die bitch" on Gabby's letter, and "die cops."

Around two A.M. on January 8, Bryce Tierney was watching television when his cell phone rang. He didn't answer, and the call went to voice mail. It said: "Hey, this is Jared. Um, we had some good times together. Uh, see you later." Later, Tierney would say the message sounded suicidal.

* * *

After the Walmart clerk turned down Jared Loughner's first attempt to buy bullets, he tried a Super Walmart in nearby Marana. At 7:27 he was able to buy eight boxes of bullets for eighty-three dollars. Federal law regulates the sale of ammunition, but it does not require a background check at the time of purchase. Neither the store, the state, nor the federal government restricts the amount of ammunition one can buy. Loughner also purchased a black backpack-style diaper bag.

On his way home, Loughner ran a red light under an overpass and drifted into the intersection.

Alen Forney, a state game and fish officer, was right behind

Loughner's Chevy Nova. Forney switched on his emergency lights. Loughner stopped on the other side of the intersection. Forney called in the license plate. He pulled behind Loughner, approached the car, and surveyed the interior.

Loughner took off his black beanie and handed his driver's license and registration to Forney through the window.

"I suppose you know why I'm stopping you," he said.

All of Loughner's paperwork checked out. No warrants, no arrests. Forney was eager to join other game and fish officers for an off-road patrol, and his department doesn't give many traffic tickets. He had no reason to check the trunk. Loughner kept his hands on the steering wheel and gave no reason for Forney to be suspicious.

Forney gave Loughner the lecture about running red lights. "It's bad for your health. You're gonna kill someone. You're gonna kill yourself." He told Loughner he was going to give him a citation rather than a ticket. The young man's face screwed up and he started to cry.

"Are you okay?" Forney asked.

"I've just had a rough time," Loughner said. "I'm okay. I just thought you were going to give me a ticket." Forney asked if he was sure he could drive. "Can I thank you?" Loughner asked.

"Sure," the officer responded.

Loughner stuck his hand out and shook Forney's. He said he was driving home. Forney gave him his paperwork and said: "Be safe."

*　*　*

Amy and Randy Loughner saw their son drive up around 8:30. Randy Loughner had returned from the store a few minutes earlier with a newspaper and a cup of coffee.

When he got out of the car, Jared Loughner had something in his hand. His mother thought it might have been a cell phone or an iPod. He walked around, opened the trunk, pulled out his black backpack, and walked into the house.

His mother said good morning and asked what he had in the backpack. His father thought he was acting strange.

"What are you up to?" Amy Loughner asked.

Jared Loughner didn't respond. He ran out of the door.

Randy Loughner chased him. He dropped his coffee. He couldn't catch his son, who disappeared down Soledad Street, the new black backpack over his shoulder.

The backpack contained the Glock 19 with a fully loaded thirty-three-round magazine and three more magazines, two of the fifteen-round variety and an additional magazine with thirty-three rounds.

* * *

Gabby's staff arrived at the Safeway a few minutes before nine A.M. to set up for Congress on Your Corner.

Gabe Zimmerman knew the drill. This would be his twenty-first meet-and-greet event. Gabe was one of Gabby's favorite people, almost like a little brother. He was tall and athletic and had worked on her first campaign for Congress in 2006, then joined her staff and became her community outreach director. He had grown up in Tucson and shared her love for hiking the mountains. Gabe was a champion problem solver and peacemaker. He would go to great lengths to address constituents' concerns and make them feel appreciated along the way. His boundless positive energy set the tone for Gabby's Tucson office. His colleagues called him the Constituent Whisperer. Everyone adored Gabe, especially his fiancée, Kelly O'Brien, a nurse in Tucson.

Pam Simon arrived to help out, too. Like Gabe Zimmerman, she was Gabby's friend and staff member. She was close enough to Gabby that she would keep Gabby's refrigerator stocked and ready for when she returned from Washington. Daniel Hernandez, who had just joined the staff as an intern, came to help set up tables and stock them with pamphlets and brochures. Sarah Hummel Rajca arrived to lend a hand. She worked on solar-energy issues for Gabby and also served as the staff photographer.

By 9:45, the team was almost ready. They had arranged two tables in an L shape: one with its end against the Safeway's brick wall, the second lengthwise along the parking lot, parallel to the Safeway. There was a space between the tables so people could chat with Gabby and walk out behind her. It was a cool and sunny morning but windy, so the staff used rocks to weigh down paperwork and brochures. They strung a GABRIELLE GIFFORDS banner between two brick pillars. They set up two flagpoles, one with a US flag, the other with an Arizona flag. They arranged white folding chairs with blue cushions along the Safeway's brick wall so constituents could sit while waiting their turn to speak with Gabby. They stretched a rope a few feet in front of the chairs to keep the line organized.

* * *

Shortly after nine A.M., Jared Loughner walked into a Circle K convenience store in his neighborhood. He asked the clerk to call a taxi for him. At first Loughner stood quietly by the register as the clerk phoned the cab company, then he started to pace.

"Are they coming?" he asked.

He walked in and out of the store and went to the bathroom a few times. At one point he took a plastic Ziploc baggie from his back pocket. It contained some cash, a credit card, and his ID. He asked the clerk to change a dollar bill into quarters.

The clerk noticed him walking around the store and mumbling to himself. At one point he looked at the clock and said: "It's nine twenty-five. I still have time."

A yellow cab pulled up fifteen minutes later at 9:40. Loughner got in the back and directed the driver to the Safeway at Casas Adobes.

* * *

Matt Laos, an Army reservist, arrived at the Safeway about a half hour early. He helped Gabe Zimmerman and Daniel Hernandez set up. He had come to discuss deficit reduction and voice his support for Gabby's proposal that members of Congress take a 5 percent pay cut. Recently returned from Afghanistan, Laos wanted to show Gabby the certificate for the medal he had received. He signed up to be first in line. The last picture taken of Gabby before she was shot was with Matt.

Jim and Doris Tucker came to meet Gabby and talk about her work at the University of Arizona. Gabby had helped fund solar research for her department. Jim, a former firefighter, worked for Raytheon, an aerospace and defense company. Neighbors knew him as "the gentle bear." They signed up to be second.

Mavanell "Mavy" Stoddard and her husband, Dory, showed up to discuss immigration. They were impressed that Gabby had been talking to ranchers on the Mexican border and wanted to lend their support. Driving toward the Safeway, they considered having breakfast first. At the last minute they turned in to the Safeway parking lot to go straight to the event.

Carol and Ken Dorushka were about tenth in line. They had come to the Safeway to do some shopping and figured they would take the opportunity to meet Gabby first. Ken wanted to thank her for supporting health care reform. He had lost his insurance but would get coverage under the new law. They were standing and talking about health care with a couple who were next in line.

George Morris, a former Marine, came with his wife of fifty-five years, Doris, to convince Gabby to take more conservative positions. He and another man with more liberal views had gotten into a heated conversation in the parking lot, but Gabe Zimmerman stepped in to defuse it.

Roger and Faith Salzgeber were Gabby Giffords fans. Roger had logged about thirty hours volunteering for her last campaign. The couple wanted to congratulate Gabby on her reelection and offer to pitch in for her next campaign.

Suzi Hileman had picked up Christina-Taylor Green, her neighbor's nine-year-old daughter, at about 9:45. Christina had a budding interest in politics, and Hileman had offered to take her to the Congress on Your Corner to meet Gabby. On the short ride to the Safeway, Christina sat in the front seat and prepared a question about the oil spill in the Gulf and how the government could help protect the environment. When they arrived, Christina was the youngest in line by far, and quickly became the star of the show.

By then Gabby had arrived. Hileman pointed her out. "Christina," Hileman said, "this could be you someday."

Retired Army colonel Bill Badger, seventy-four, came to the event just to visit with Gabby. He was another fan. Patricia Maisch would describe herself the same way. She stood in line to thank Gabby for supporting the economic stimulus plan. It had allowed her to hire more workers for the heating and cooling company she ran with her husband.

Phyllis Schneck, seventy-nine, came to Tucson every winter from her home in New Jersey. A Republican, she came to discuss immigration and border security with Gabby. Tom McMahon and Mary Reed stood near the back of the line with their two teenage children. Their daughter had served as a congressional page for Gabby the previous summer but had not had a chance to meet her. She thought Gabby was a rock star.

Mary Reed was deep in conversation with Ken Veeder, a retired Vietnam veteran who had survived three tours in the Airborne Infantry Division. At seventy-five, he had close-cropped gray hair and a craggy face. He had come to ask for Gabby's assistance in resolving a dispute with the Veterans Affairs department in Phoenix. When Mary Reed heard that Veeder was a paratrooper in Vietnam who had lived through three tours, she asked if she could rub him for good luck.

"Sure," he said.

Gabby parked her old Toyota 4Runner SUV by the grocery-cart enclosure and walked toward the Safeway entrance. She could see about twenty people lined up, sitting, standing, or talking.

Ron Barber, her district director and the man who ran the Tucson office, arrived about the same time. They met in the parking lot. Gabby gave him a hug.

"Let's do this," she said.

Before Gabby could begin meeting constituents, she had to hug staffers she hadn't seen for weeks. One for Gabe Zimmerman, another for Pam Simon and Sara Hummel Rajca, and one for Daniel Hernandez, the new intern.

Matt Laos, the reservist, stepped up. Gabby wanted to give him a hug but he was too shy. They talked about a soldier they both knew who had been killed in Afghanistan. They discussed how her proposal to cut congressional pay might cost each member $8,700, and Gabby made a few jokes. They posed for a picture, and Laos left through the space between the two tables.

As Jim and Doris Tucker stepped forward to talk about solar energy with Gabby, Ron Barber saw John Roll approach from the parking lot. Roll, Arizona's chief federal judge, had been close to Gabby for years. She had made a point of meeting with him and other judges when she first took office, and they had become friends.

"Hi, Ron," he said. "I just wanted to say hello to the congresswoman. I'll come back."

Roll was on the other side of the table that stood between the parking lot and Gabby, with Barber by her side. Barber knew that Gabby had written a letter on Roll's behalf to help settle a matter with California judges. "Come on around," Barber told Roll. "As soon as she's finished with these constituents, I know she'll want to talk with you."

Roll joined Gabby and Ron, their backs against the Safeway.

* * *

Jared Loughner could see the back of Gabby's head through the window from inside the Safeway.

He had arrived at the supermarket around 9:45. He had a twenty-dollar bill in the plastic bag in his back pocket and needed change to pay the cabbie. He convinced the driver to walk into the Safeway with him to get change, a transaction they completed at the customer-service desk.

Loughner bought a bottle of water and then walked through the aisles. Surveillance video inside the store shows him using some sort of sign language to the cashier as he purchased the water. The woman at the register didn't seem to pay attention to these odd gestures. He walked around the aisles, occasionally coming toward the front of the store, where he is seen glancing in Gabby's direction on the other side of the glass. At about ten he left the Safeway and walked around the line of constituents to the table with literature. Alex Villec, one of Gabby's volunteers, was greeting people from behind the table.

"Can I talk to the congresswoman?" Loughner asked Villec. "It's just a routine question."

Gabby was standing behind Villec, in conversation with Jim and Doris Tucker. Ron Barber was by her side. Judge Roll waited behind Barber. Pam Simon stood a few steps away.

"Sure," Villec said. "You have to go to the back of the line. She'll be with you in fifteen or twenty minutes."

Loughner seemed standoffish and different. Villec had worked a few of these events for Gabby. They didn't often draw young men in hoodies who looked like they were dressed for clubbing or hanging out on a street corner.

Loughner didn't respond. He turned and walked to the back of the line. Gabby's intern, Daniel Hernandez, handed a clipboard to Loughner and asked him to sign in.

Less than a minute later, Loughner rushed to the front tables, a few feet from where Gabby was standing with her back to the Safeway. His face was stone cold. He had inserted orange plugs in his ears. He barged through the opening between the tables, raised his right hand, and pointed his 9mm Glock directly at Gabby Giffords's head. Then he started to shoot.

"Gun!" someone yelled.

* * *

Gabby turned toward Loughner, who was now right in front of her. He fired his gun from point-blank range, hitting Gabby above her left eye. Her legs buckled as she was propelled backward against the brick wall and window. She slumped to the ground.

Waving the Glock and squeezing the trigger, Loughner shot Judge Roll, Ron Barber, and Pam Simon. The judge dropped to the sidewalk, stood up, and fell dead. Gabe Zimmerman heard the popping and ran toward Gabby. Loughner shot him once. He fell between Gabby and Barber.

Still swinging the Glock slowly, Loughner turned toward the people in line. He shot Jim Tucker in the shoulder and calf. His wife, Doris, covered her ears. Loughner missed her. She saw her husband on the ground with others who had been shot.

Dory Stoddard shoved his wife, Mavy, down and covered her with his body. Loughner lowered the Glock and shot him in the back. Mavy felt the bullet that killed her husband. She sat up, cradled her husband's head in her lap, and yelled: "Help me! Help me!" She didn't realize Loughner had shot her in the legs.

Loughner moved quickly down the line of constituents. He kept squeezing off rounds. It sounded like the popping of firecrackers. Loughner wounded George Morris. He killed Dorothy, Morris's wife of fifty-five years. He shot and killed Phyllis Schneck.

He shot young Christina-Taylor Green in the chest. Suzi Hileman instinctively turned toward Christina, who looked her in the eye. Hileman looked down and saw a bullet hole in her own thigh, one of three.

Mary Reed heard the popping sound. She realized it was gunfire. She stood up, pinned her daughter against the Safeway wall, and covered her up. She raised her arms. Loughner shot her in the back and arms.

Loughner fired thirty-three rounds in about fifteen seconds. Then silence.

*　*　*

Retired Army colonel Bill Badger heard the gunfire and ducked. He felt a bullet graze the back of his head. It burned. He looked up and saw Jared Loughner heading directly at him, firing.

Someone raised a folding chair to smash Loughner. He ducked to absorb the blow. Loughner's gun was now out of bullets. He reached into his pocket for more ammunition, but he fumbled with the second thirty-three-round magazine, and it fell to the ground.

Bill Badger rushed him, grabbed his left arm, and forced him to the pavement.

Roger Salzgeber had heard what he thought were fireworks, but then he saw blood on the ground. As Loughner rushed past, Salzgeber's wife, Faith, tumbled back in the melee. Neither was hit. Salzgeber ran after Loughner, saw him on the ground, put his knee on his neck, wrapped his right arm behind his back, and pulled.

"Ow, ow!" Loughner said. "You're hurting me."

Pat Maisch had dropped to the ground when she heard the shooting. She did not get hit. She saw Loughner try to reload, but now he was on the ground. A magazine lay by his side. She grabbed it so he couldn't reload and sat on his legs.

Ken Veeder, the Vietnam vet, knew the pop-pop-pop was the sound of gunfire, not firecrackers. He saw Loughner shooting and running toward him. He saw Mary Reed cover her daughter and get shot in the back. Veeder took a bullet to the leg. As Loughner went down and his gun fell to the ground, Veeder grabbed it.

"Give me the magazine," he told Maisch. "I'm going to shoot the son of a bitch."

Maisch refused and urged Veeder to calm down.

Joe Zamudio had been buying cigarettes in the Walgreens next to the Safeway when he heard the shots. He was legally carrying a concealed weapon and had a handgun in his pocket. Zamudio, twenty-four, grabbed the handle of his pistol but kept it in his pocket. He rushed out, prepared to draw and fire. He saw Loughner pinned down and a man holding the Glock.

"Put the gun down," Zamudio said. He grabbed Veeder's wrist and sat on Loughner.

Veeder dropped the Glock. Zamudio later said in an interview: "I almost killed that guy"—meaning Veeder, who had grabbed Loughner's gun. Amid the chaos of the moment, the shooting was nearly capped off with a terrible accident where the "good guy with a gun," with the best of intentions, could have killed an innocent bystander.

"Just keep your feet on it," Zamudio said. "We'll all be safe."

Pima County sheriffs arrived within minutes. Deputy Sheriff Thomas Audetat saw Maisch, Zamudio, and Salzgeber holding Loughner down. He put his knee on Loughner, cuffed him, and searched him. He found two fully loaded magazines in one pocket and a folding knife in another. Audetat took him into custody. In the backseat of the patrol car on the way to the sheriff's office, Loughner said one thing:

"I just want you to know that I'm the only person that knew about this."

* * *

Ron Barber, Gabby's district director, lay wounded under the table.

Loughner had shot Barber in the face and leg. Pam Simon was down, too, hit in the wrist and chest. Barber could see Gabe Zimmerman lying still by his side; Loughner had killed his friend Gabe. A woman kneeled by Barber and applied pressure to the wound in his leg.

Barber could see Gabby, her head against the wall and her back to him. He knew Loughner had shot her first. Daniel Hernandez, who had done some training as a nursing assistant, kneeled down and took Barber's pulse. Barber told him to stay by Gabby.

Gabby's eyes were closed, though she had a strong pulse and was conscious. Hernandez propped her up, held her head in his arm, and applied pressure to her wound to stop the bleeding. He asked her to squeeze his hand. Her right side was limp, but she squeezed his finger with her left hand.

David and Nancy Bowman had been shopping in the Safeway when they heard the sound of gunfire. David is a doctor, Nancy a nurse. They ran out and immediately began basic triage to the fallen: checking their pulses and alertness and evaluating their injuries.

Nancy came upon Suzi Hileman trying to tend to Christina-Taylor Green.

"Suzi," she said, "you have to lay down. We're taking care of Christina. You need to take care of yourself."

*　*　*

At 10:11, the minute after Loughner had opened fire, the Pima County Sheriff's Department started receiving 911 calls. Three minutes later, Rural Metro Fire Rescue dispatched the first paramedic unit to the scene. Four minutes after the first call, Deputy Sheriff Thomas Audetat arrived at the Safeway and detained Loughner. Medical personnel rolled in at 10:19, but they held back a few minutes so police could secure the area. Three fire engines and three ambulances got the all-clear at 10:22 and sped to the victims. A second alarm brought more fire engines, seven more ambulances, and three helicopters.

Colt Jackson was the first paramedic to treat Gabby. When he reached the scene, he saw several bodies already covered in sheets. People were doing CPR on Christina-Taylor Green. A triage officer pointed to Gabby and told Jackson to take care of her. Daniel Hernandez was still holding her.

"What's going on?" Jackson asked.

"This is Gabrielle Giffords," Hernandez said. "She's been shot in the head."

Colt Jackson moved Hernandez's arm away so he could examine Gabby. He saw the gunshot wound and the blood. She couldn't respond, but she was breathing. She couldn't open her eyes or talk, but she reached out with her left hand and grabbed his fingers.

Jackson put a cervical collar on her neck and placed an oxygen mask over her mouth. He strapped her to a board and planned to fly her to a hospital, but the choppers had not arrived. An ambulance rushed her to University Medical Center. The ambulance departed at 10:41 and arrived at the hospital thirteen minutes later. Hernandez stayed by her side until she arrived in the emergency room.

Paramedics kept trying CPR on Christina-Taylor Green. She didn't respond. They rushed her to the hospital, where trauma surgeon Dr. Randy Friese operated on her so they could massage her heart. He could not revive her.

Loughner had left thirteen wounded. Five people were declared dead at the scene: Gabe Zimmerman, Judge Roll, Dory Stoddard, Dorothy Morris, and Phyllis Schneck. Christina was the sixth.

* * *

On the morning of January 8, I was at home in Houston with my daughters. Claire was sleeping in and Claudia and I were talking when the phone rang. It was Gabby's chief of staff, Pia Carusone, calling from Washington to say that my wife had been shot. That was all she knew. I took the news calmly, in total shock, and ended the call within thirty seconds.

The news seemed so horrific and unbelievable that, a minute after hanging up with Pia, I pressed redial. "Tell me again," I said, and Pia confirmed that I had not imagined the whole nightmare.

I immediately called Gabby's parents in Tucson. Spencer started sobbing as soon as I delivered the devastating news. Gloria, who was at a UPS store, reacted with the numbness I had displayed.

I had to get to Tucson right away—but how? A commercial flight would've taken too long, and I was in no state to fly myself in one of NASA's T-38s. (In any event, because it was Saturday, the planes were unavailable.) Then I thought of my friend Tilman Fertitta, a restaurant and casino owner who had his own planes.

Tilman acted fast, and within the hour, my daughters, mother, and I were en route to the airport. During the excruciating two-and-a-half-hour flight that followed, we heard several news reports that Gabby had died. The media was wrong, thank God, but I will never get back those terrible minutes of my life when I was forced to confront the worst.

Loughner's bullet had fractured Gabby's skull, passed through her brain, and fractured the top of both of her eye sockets. Neurosurgeon Dr. Martin Weinand operated on her almost as soon as she arrived at the hospital. Doctors removed the left side of her skull to relieve the pressure caused by the swelling of her brain. When we reached University Medical Center, Gabby was out of surgery. Gloria and Spencer were already there. Doctors ushered us into a private room and described her condition and what they had tried to accomplish.

"Your wife is going to survive," chief trauma surgeon Peter Rhee said. "But beyond that, we don't know much."

UMC was like a military hospital in Iraq or Afghanistan that day. Ron Barber was in the intensive care unit, recovering from wounds to the face and leg. The hospital treated a dozen of the wounded, with injuries ranging from Bill Badger's head wound to Mavy Stoddard's shot-up legs.

Gabby was in a coma for a week. By January 19, she was able to stand with the help of medical staff. By February 9, a month after the shooting, she was able to speak a little. She even asked for toast for breakfast.

To be shot in the head from just a few feet away and survive is rare. That's an understatement: Gabby's recovery has been nothing short of miraculous.

She would live to mourn, to love, to fight—and to face Jared Lee Loughner.

CHAPTER FOUR

"YOU FAILED!"

For more than a year after the shooting, Gabby showed no interest in Jared Lee Loughner: who he was, what his motive had been, what would become of him in the future.

We had zero time or patience to obsess about his path through the criminal justice system, but Wally Kleindienst, the federal prosecutor assigned to the case, filled us in on each development.

Within days of the shooting, prosecutors charged Loughner with five criminal counts, including attempted assassination of a member of Congress. Police had searched his room and found a note in an envelope in his safe where he'd written about the "assassination" and, also, "I planned ahead." Despite initial reports to the contrary, they determined he had acted alone.

In March 2011, a federal grand jury indicted Loughner on forty-nine counts, including multiple charges for murder, assault, and the attempted assassination of a congresswoman. He faced being sentenced to many life terms; he was also eligible for the death penalty. Loughner appeared in court on March 9, flashed a crazy grin, and pleaded not guilty. He was confined at the time in maximum-security prisons in Phoenix and Tucson.

The court appointed Judy Clarke to represent him. We welcomed the news. She was a top-notch defense lawyer who had represented "Unabomber" Ted Kaczynski and Olympic bomber Eric Rudolph. Even the man who shot my wife and killed six innocent people deserves a competent lawyer, and having Clarke in the role was in the best interest of the prosecution as well. We wanted him to have a very good attorney so the process wouldn't get screwed up.

No federal judges from Arizona could rule on the Loughner case, since they had worked alongside Gabby's friend Judge Roll, so California federal judge Larry Burns was appointed to oversee the case. On March 22, Judge Burns ordered that Loughner be transferred to the US Medical Center for Federal Prisoners in Springfield, Missouri, where psychiatrists could evaluate him.

Two months later, on May 22, Burns held a hearing in Tucson to decide whether Loughner was competent to stand trial. Loughner walked into court wearing shackles and looking haggard. Stubble covered his shaved head, his sideburns were long, and he slumped in his chair and rocked back and forth. Two psychiatrists testified he was delusional and spoke nonsense. Christina Pietz, a psychiatrist with the Bureau of Prisons, diagnosed schizophrenia.

Loughner didn't help his case. During the hearing, he thrashed in his chains and told the court he had succeeded in his designs on Gabby: "Thank you for the freak show. She died right in front of me. You are treasonous."

US Marshals carried Loughner from the courtroom.

"At the present time," Judge Burns said, "Mr. Loughner does not have a rational understanding of these proceedings." He ruled that Loughner was not competent to stand trial. For the next year, doctors at his Missouri mental facility forced Loughner to take medications. The treatment gradually restored some presence of mind to him. By the summer of 2012, Dr. Pietz said he had begun to comprehend the violence he had wrought and the consequences of his actions. Prosecutors entered into negotiations for a plea agreement with Loughner that would avoid a trial, yet put him away for the rest of his life.

The prosecutors then came to Gabby and me for our opinion. Would we be satisfied with a deal that would spare Loughner from the death penalty? Gabby and I talked it over.

"No death penalty," she said.

Since becoming an elected official and studying the issue, Gabby had changed her stance on capital punishment. She used to be in favor of the death penalty, but after seeing dozens of death-row inmates released after they were later found to be innocent, she had changed her mind. I had my own problems with the death penalty. In addition to the finality of the punishment, there is also the cost: it is often more expensive than life in prison. And I don't always think it is the worst punishment. In Loughner's case, I wanted him to have decades to contemplate what he had done. In my view, spending the rest of his days locked up behind bars was worse punishment than execution. Prosecutors also asked everyone whose loved ones had died for their opinions on the death penalty in the case. We believe that most families agreed that they should not pursue it.

At a hearing on August 7, 2012, Judge Burns ruled that Loughner had gained enough sense to stand trial. Dr. Pietz, the forensic psychiatrist who had diagnosed Loughner with schizophrenia, testified that he was a changed individual. He had expressed remorse to her, especially for the murder of Christina-Taylor Green, which he said was not intentional.

In his attempted assassination of Gabby, though, Loughner remained despondent. He was so certain he had killed
her, and the reality that she had survived took him months
to comprehend and accept. As is the case with most assassins,
he was trying to accomplish one goal: to become famous for
committing a heinous crime against a public figure.

That same day, he pleaded guilty to nineteen counts.
Under a plea agreement, he was facing life in prison without
parole. But the death penalty was off the table.

Judge Burns scheduled a sentencing hearing for November 8.

"Do you want to go?" I asked Gabby.

"No," she said.

*   *   *

As Loughner's case wound its way through the criminal justice system, Gabby was working day and night to recover
from the gunshot to her head. In many ways, Gabby's progress had been faster and more successful than her doctors
and the medical specialists had expected. "Miraculous,"
they said. But in tunneling through her brain, the bullet
had caused lasting harm. It paralyzed much of the right side
of her body: she struggled to walk, her right arm was completely paralyzed, and she has no right-side peripheral vision
out of either eye.

Before the shooting, Gabby had been a gifted speaker
who loved the give-and-take of talking with friends and
colleagues. She could deliver impassioned speeches on the
House floor. She loved to talk for hours with me, her staffers, her friends. She was a voracious reader. Loughner's bullet robbed her of the ability to communicate well. He left her
with aphasia: she could form thoughts but could not easily

communicate them. She had a hard time quickly forming complete sentences. She could understand everything said around her, but she would often only respond with a few words, or a sentence or two.

From the very beginning, Gabby has worked tirelessly to improve: doing speech-therapy sessions every week, writing on her iPad, chatting with me and her colleagues.

These days, when my wife and I drive through Tucson for a night out or to visit friends, Gabby sits in the front passenger seat to my right. She offers me her left hand; we hold hands until I need both on the wheel. Whenever I walk into a room, Gabby still flashes me that trademark smile, beckons me over, and kisses me on the head, as if she hadn't seen me for a week. She still criticizes my wardrobe relentlessly. One day I asked her if I was dressed well for an interview. I wore a jacket over a T-shirt.

"No, no, no," she said. "A blouse."

She meant a shirt. I changed.

* * *

While Gabby devoted herself to making a full recovery, life in Washington, DC, continued on its dysfunctional course.

On the last day of July 2011, with the eyes of the nation anxiously watching, President Obama and House Speaker John Boehner reached an agreement to ensure that our government could pay its bills. But their deal had to pass the House. If it failed, the government would default, and the economy could crash.

Gabby, who was still serving as a congresswoman, followed the acrimonious debate with great interest and concern. The constant combat between the parties always troubled her. At the time, we were living in Houston, so her staffs in Washington and Tucson ran the day-to-day congressional operations: staying in touch with Gabby, serving constituents, putting out press releases. Gabby was trying to serve from afar.

As the day of the debt vote drew near, Gabby's Democratic colleagues gave her regular updates; a few said it might come down to a single vote. Before bed that night, we talked. "They might need your vote in Washington tomorrow," I said. "What do you think?"

"I don't know," she answered.

It wasn't until the day of the vote that she made the decision: she was going to go to Washington to cast her vote. But it wouldn't be easy; getting from Texas to the House floor proved to be a major undertaking. Gabby had to transform herself in a day from a brain-injury patient who wore comfortable clothes to a congresswoman looking the part of a representative prepared to cast a vote. She had not been to Washington since the shooting. To make the trip and the vote, she would need new clothes (she had lost so much weight since the shooting that her old wardrobe no longer fit) and shoes, too, since her right foot and leg didn't work like they used to. More than that, Gabby needed two nurses, her entire staff on alert, her "112th Congress" pin, and her official House of Representatives voting card. We managed to get organized, with much help from her staff and friends. We took a commercial flight that got us into Reagan National Airport just after five P.M.

Later that evening, Gabby walked slowly across the House floor, her hair still short because of the brain surgery. As she cast her vote, her colleagues broke out in cheers—and tears. Vice President Joe Biden had rushed over when he heard she might be there.

President Obama invited her to the White House.

"No," Gabby said. "Back to work."

"In Congress?" I asked.

"No, no," she said. "Rehab."

* * *

Gabby and I occasionally talked about whether she wanted to continue serving in Congress. True, she was improving steadily, but she came to the conclusion that she couldn't dedicate herself to her recovery and still serve her constituents well. On Sunday, January 22, 2012, just over a year after being shot, she announced in a video she would step down.

"Thank you for your prayers and for giving me time to recover," she said. "I have more work to do on my recovery, so to do what is best for Arizona, I will step down this week."

But she also said: "I will return, and we will work together for Arizona and this great country."

But what did that mean exactly? At the time, not even the people closest to Gabby knew which work she would choose. We spent the bulk of the next year discussing how she could best serve her country outside of elected office.

In the meantime, Gabby kept her spirits up and her mind focused on regaining her ability to communicate. In the fall of 2012, she picked up her iPhone for the first time and dialed up her best friend, Raoul.

"Dinner?" she asked.

What was a simple task for us was yet another breakthrough for Gabby.

They would keep coming.

* * *

81

A month before Loughner's November 8, 2012, sentencing hearing, I again asked Gabby if she wanted to attend. The prosecutors had been calling. They said many of the victims and those who had lost loved ones would have a chance to address Loughner. Gabby was still undecided.

"This will be our one and only chance to tell him face-to-face the consequences of what he did that day," I said. "Don't you want to show him that you are alive and well, that you prevailed and that he failed?"

She looked at me with troubled eyes. Gabby and I often don't have to speak to communicate. I could tell she was thinking about Gabe, Judge Roll, Christina-Taylor, and the other victims. She looked down for a moment, and then she reached out to hold my hand.

"Okay, let's go," she said.

The morning of the sentencing, prosecutors sent a car for us. My daughters Claudia and Claire piled in, and we were all driven to the courthouse.

Gabby's mom, Gloria, declined; she still couldn't face the man who had shot her daughter in the head. And she, like the rest of us, was also struggling with the loss of Spencer, Gabby's dad and Gloria's husband of forty-seven years. Spencer had been in poor health for some years, but his death in late October had been sudden and unexpected. He died in the middle of the night, with no warning; Gloria found him when she woke up the next morning. It was a devastating loss at an already emotional time.

The hearing was scheduled to begin at ten A.M. We arrived at the federal courthouse in Tucson at 9:30 to meet briefly with Judge Burns and the prosecutor Wally Kleindienst. In the courtroom, I approached Judy Clarke and thanked her for representing Loughner. Gabby and I took seats in the second row. Many of Gabby's staff members from Washington and Tucson arrived and filled the seats behind us. Almost every person who had come to see Gabby that day outside the Safeway—or their surviving family members—was there to witness Loughner's sentencing.

Just before Judge Burns gaveled the room to order, Amy and Randy Loughner arrived. They sat in the first row on the defense side. Gabby and I didn't feel a pressing desire to talk with them, but we would not have turned away had they approached us. We never spoke.

Gabby nudged me when marshals escorted Jared Loughner to the defense table. It was the first time she had laid eyes on the man. He was wearing a dark shirt, a tie, and brown pants, rather than the orange prison suit he had worn to previous court sessions. His brown hair was cut short. His face wore a blank expression. He seemed composed but troubled. To me, he looked small and diminished.

Christina Pietz, Loughner's principal psychiatrist, spoke first. She told the court that she treated Loughner almost every day at the federal prison in Missouri.

"It's my opinion Mr. Loughner is competent to stand trial," she testified.

Judy Clarke agreed and said he continued to show improvement. Her client kept his eyes lowered to the table and his hands in his lap. Clarke indicated that Loughner did not wish to address the court. Judge Burns wanted to make sure and asked him directly.

"That is true," Loughner said in a deep tone that was long, drawn out, and sounded forced. It sounded like it was difficult for him to get the words out.

* * *

83

For the better part of the next hour, victims and witnesses walked to the front of the courtroom and spoke their hearts and minds.

Pat Maisch spoke first. Though she had not been physically injured, her perspective and her role in helping subdue Loughner had made her one of the most persistent and thoughtful voices.

"That beautiful day," Maisch said, "our mental health system failed us. For six, that failure was devastating and unimaginable." Maisch was not the only one to assign blame to the mental health system. As I listened, I couldn't keep from wondering what might have stopped Loughner from his horrific actions. So many what-ifs.

I glanced over at his parents. They had known their son was suffering, not connecting, diving deeper into a disturbed mental state. He was living under their roof. They tried to help him, but could they have done more? What if Randy Loughner had caught up with his son that Saturday morning and looked inside his black backpack?

His friends knew that he was unstable and in possession of a lethal weapon. Could they at least have alerted his parents?

Upon expelling Loughner, Pima Community College had stated that a mental examination would be required before he was readmitted and advised his parents to keep guns away from him. But what if the college had shared that information with law enforcement? Might it have affected his background check when he bought the Glock?

Why was it so easy for Loughner to buy the high-capacity magazines? The same question was on Judge Burns's mind. Later in the hearing he said: "I don't understand the social utility of allowing citizens to have magazines with thirty bullets."

* * *

Suzi Hileman could not hold back her anger as she faced Loughner and told him how he had killed Christina-Taylor Green. "We brought friends and children," she said. "You brought a gun." And: "You turned a civics lesson into a nightmare."

Mavy Stoddard brought tears to our eyes when she told Loughner how she felt when he shot and killed her husband, Dory. "You took away my life, my love, my reason for living. I am so lonesome," Stoddard said. She stared directly at Loughner. "I hate living without him. No one to hold me, no one to love me, no one to talk to, no one to care. I forgive you. As a Christian, I am required to."

I could see Amy Loughner weeping, too.

Ron Barber could not bring himself to forgive Loughner, but he said he "held no hatred" for the man.

Barber was Gabby's district director at the time of the shooting. He had recovered from the bullet wound to his leg. In a special election earlier that summer, Ron had run for and won Gabby's congressional seat. He brought us back to that horrible day.

"The physical and mental wounds will be with us forever," Barber said. And then he talked about Gabe Zimmerman.

"He was my go-to guy," he said of Gabe, "a human being with so much compassion. I will never forget seeing him die by my side."

Ron turned to look at Gabby.

"We are thankful she survived your attempt to take her life," Barber told Loughner. "You did not take away her compassion and desire to serve. In fact, the whole world knows of this great leader. She remains the model of bipartisanship and political courage."

* * *

Gabby and I spoke last. We approached the bench together.

"May we address the defendant directly?" I asked Judge Burns. He said yes, so we stepped to the side of the podium and turned to face Jared Loughner. He was about twenty feet away. We stared at him; he looked back.

For months after his rampage, Loughner was convinced he had succeeded in assassinating Gabby. Many of his early outbursts, in particular the one in open court, came about because his lawyer or his psychiatrist told him Gabby had survived.

Now he could see her staring right into his eyes.

As I spoke, Gabby didn't once look away.

"Mr. Loughner," I began, "for the first and last time, you are going to hear directly from Gabby and me about what you took away on January 8th, 2011, and, just as important, what you did not. So pay attention."

Gabby and I had worked together on our statement, but I would deliver it. We stood shoulder to shoulder.

"That bright and chilly Saturday morning," I said, "you killed six innocent people. Daughters and sons. Mothers and fathers. Grandparents and friends. They were devoted to their families, their communities, their places of worship.

"Gabby would trade her own life to bring back any one of those you savagely murdered on that day. Especially young Christina-Taylor Green, whose high-minded ideas about service and democracy deserved a full life committed to advancing them.

"Especially thirty-year-old Gabe Zimmerman, whom

Gabby knew well and cherished, and whose love for his family and his fiancée and service to his country were as deep as his loss is tragic. Especially Judge John Roll, whom Gabby was honored to call a colleague and friend and from whose interminable dedication to our community and country she gained enormous inspiration. Gabby would give anything to take away the grief you visited upon the Morrises, the Schnecks, and the Stoddards—anything to heal the bodies and psyches of your other victims."

Gabby nodded. She never took her eyes from Loughner.

"And then there is what you took from Gabby," I continued. "Her life has been forever changed. Plans she had for our family and her career have been immeasurably altered."

I paused for a moment, and a sudden memory hit me—the baby we were trying to have at exactly the time Loughner shot Gabby.

"Every day is a continuous struggle to do those things she was once so very good at," I said. "Now she struggles to deliver each and every sentence. Her gift for language can now only be seen in Internet videos from a more innocent time.

"Gabby was an outdoor enthusiast. She was often seen Rollerblading with her friend Raoul in Reed Park, hiking in Sabino Canyon, or careening down Rillito Wash Trail on her bike, as she was the night before you tried and failed to murder her. She hasn't been to any of those places since, and I don't know when she'll return.

"There's more. Gabby struggles to walk. Her right arm is paralyzed. She is partially blind. Gabby works harder in one minute of an hour—fighting to make each individual moment count for something—than most of us work in an entire day."

Not a sound in the courtroom.

"Mr. Loughner," I continued, "by making death and producing tragedy, you sought to extinguish the beauty of life. To diminish potential. To strain love. And to cancel ideas. You tried to create for all of us a world as dark and evil as your own. But know this, and remember it always: you failed."

At that we paused to let it sink in. Loughner looked down.

In the weeks leading up to the sentencing hearing, Gabby and I had begun to discuss the politics of gun legislation. In writing our statement, we agreed the time had come to start going public.

"Your decision to commit cold-blooded mass murder also begs of us to look in the mirror," I said. "This horrific act warns us to hold our leaders and ourselves responsible for coming up short when we do, for not having the courage to act when it's hard, even for possessing the wrong values. We are a people who can watch a young man like you spiral into murderous rampage without choosing to intervene before it is too late."

And then: "We have a political class that is afraid to do something as simple as have a meaningful debate about our gun laws and how they are being enforced. We have representatives who look at gun violence not as a problem to solve but as the sleeping giant in the room to ignore. As a nation we have repeatedly passed up the opportunity to address this issue. After Columbine; after Virginia Tech; after Tucson and after Aurora we have done nothing."

We also decided to take the opportunity to speak freely about what Gabby had called the "nut jobs" in Arizona state government.

"In this state we have elected officials so feckless in their leadership that they would say, as in the case of Governor

Jan Brewer, 'I don't think it has anything to do with the size of the magazine or the caliber of the gun.' She went on and said, 'Even if the shooter's weapon had held fewer bullets, he'd have another gun, maybe. He could have three guns in his pocket'—she said this just one week after a high-capacity magazine allowed you to kill six and wound thirteen others, before being wrestled to the ground while attempting to reload. Or a state legislature that thought it appropriate to busy itself naming an official Arizona state gun just weeks after this tragedy occurred, instead of doing the work it was elected to do: encourage economic growth, help our returning veterans, and fix our education system."

These were the issues to which Gabby Giffords had dedicated her political work in state and federal government. We spoke from both frustration and anger.

Still, we wanted Loughner and the world to know that the energy and dynamism that had propelled Gabby to a successful political career were still going strong. "Mr. Loughner," I said, "you may have put a bullet through her head, but you haven't put a dent in her spirit and her commitment to make the world a better place."

As I spoke and Gabby stared at him, Loughner's facial expression ranged from disbelief—almost as if we were lying to him—to rage and confusion. But we never saw a sense of sorrow, empathy, or remorse. He still appeared to be disturbed.

"Mr. Loughner," I closed, "pay close attention to this: though you are mentally ill, you are responsible for the death and hurt you inflicted upon all of us on January 8th of last year. You know this. Gabby and I know this. Everyone in this courtroom knows this. You have decades upon decades to contemplate what you did.

"But after today," I said. "After this moment. Here and now, Gabby and I are done thinking about you."

* * *

Assistant US Attorney Wally Kleindienst said Loughner was lucky. "Almost all the victims you shot and the families of those you killed came to us and said they didn't want us to seek the death penalty in this case."

He recommended seven life sentences plus 140 years.

Loughner would remain behind bars for the remainder of his life, with no chance of parole. That gave us a sense of confidence in knowing that he would not be able to emerge in public every few years, proclaim that he had served enough time, and request release. Loughner was gone for good.

The seven life sentences were for the six people Loughner had killed plus one for the attempted assassination of a member of Congress.

Yet when Judge Burns handed down the sentence, he mentioned "six life terms."

I slipped a note to the prosecutors. "Stop the judge," I wrote. "I want to address the court right now." I explained to one of the lawyers that the judge had left Gabby out of the sentence. I wanted to make very sure she was included. Kleindienst approached the bench and spoke to the judge. Burns amended the sentence to seven life terms—and 140 years.

"This sentence provides no illusions of closure for victims," Judge Burns said. "Instead, what you get today is resolution."

Gabby and I chatted with friends and staff and hugged our way out of the courthouse.

"You okay?" I asked.

She nodded yes.

* * *

Gabby and I felt relief.

We had faced her assailant. We had imparted the essential message to his face and to the public: he was going to spend his life in jail; Gabby Giffords had survived his mayhem and was alive and well. The sentencing was another necessary step in our healing process. We could continue to emerge from this horrific time.

The legal issues were behind us.

When we finally arrived at home and could share a quiet moment, Gabby said: "I am glad. It was important for me. More important than I thought."

It was a crucial, if small, first step on our path toward changing our nation's laws on gun violence. We were surprised by how many people reacted to one particular line:

"We have a political class that is afraid to do something as simple as have a meaningful debate about our gun laws and how they are being enforced."

The "sleeping giant" in the room was beginning to stir.

CHAPTER FIVE

THE NRA:
FROM MARKSMANSHIP
TO MUSCLE

Before the Tucson shooting, Patricia Maisch never thought of herself as an activist, let alone a hero. But preventing Jared Loughner from reloading his gun had transformed her. In the aftermath of the shooting, she was moved to take action to commemorate the lives lost in the massacre.

She just wasn't sure how to go about doing that.

Maisch didn't know Gabby or me personally at the time. She had come to the Safeway that day to thank Gabby for supporting health care reform and the federal stimulus. She had always admired the stands Gabby took and saw her congresswoman as a moderate leader who could bring the country's warring political parties together. Maisch had even dreamed Gabby could be the country's first female president.

During the last weekend of April 2011, a little over four months after the shooting at the Safeway, the National Rifle Association held its annual meeting in Pittsburgh. Pat Maisch had expected to be in Tucson, helping her husband run their small heating and cooling company. But her heroic role during the shooting had raised her profile. CeaseFirePA, a coalition of Pennsylvanians fighting to reduce gun violence, asked her to join its members to march in Pittsburgh during the NRA meeting. She agreed and flew east for the weekend.

Maisch had hoped to speak with NRA leaders, but she didn't even come close. The only contact she had with an NRA member was a man who turned to the marchers and shouted, "You're not going to take our guns away!"

"We don't want your guns," Maisch responded. "We want your help."

Maisch remembers being surprised to find herself marching alongside a woman wearing a sash festooned with NRA badges: some for safety training, one for marksmanship, another for education.

"Why are you with us instead of at the convention?" Maisch asked.

"The NRA isn't what it used to be," the woman said. "We used to be a club that taught gun safety, focused on hunting, and held target-shooting competitions. Now it's more about selling guns and making money."

That was news to Pat Maisch.

* * *

It certainly wasn't news to Gabby and me. After more than a decade in elective politics, Gabby had learned all about the NRA's powerful influence in national and state politics. The organization had built a fearsome lobbying machine in Washington and in state capitals around the country. The group could raise millions of dollars to support political friends, punish enemies, and rally its membership to swing elections and votes. The NRA exercised a frightening control not only over politicians, but over gun manufacturers as well.

Some consider the NRA the most powerful lobbying group in the nation. But the woman marching with Pat Maisch was right: the NRA hadn't always been that way.

Though I'm generally not much of a joiner, I had considered becoming an NRA member when my dad gave me the Glock for graduating from flight school. Why not join an organization that helped train people to become better marksmen? I hunted occasionally and hoped to do more after leaving NASA. The NRA appealed to sportsmen, right? I did some research and discovered that that was certainly true in its early days, but less so in recent years.

Colonel William C. Church and Captain George Wingate, two high-ranking officers in the Union army, came away from the Civil War with the impression that—despite their victory—the northern troops couldn't shoot straight. That was partly true. Soldiers from farming states in New England and the Midwest knew how to aim and fire, but conscripts from the cities, many of whom were newcomers to America, were less familiar with guns. In 1871, six years after the Civil War, Church and Wingate established the National Rifle Association in an armory in Manhattan with the goal of training marksmen. The initial mission of the organization was to "promote and encourage rifle shooting on a scientific basis."

At the time, a few states had rifle associations and shooting clubs. But Church and Wingate had national ambitions. They enlisted General Ambrose Burnside, a Civil War leader whose generous facial hair gave us the term "sideburns," to be the first NRA president.

From its inception, the NRA relied on the government for money and weapons. The New York State Legislature chartered the fledgling organization and helped finance its early days. A sympathetic assemblyman pushed through a

$25,000 appropriation to buy a seventy-acre site on Long Island for an NRA rifle range. Church and Wingate sought funds from their members and asked them to send letters of support for the appropriation. They christened the new range Creedmoor.

Despite the financial boost, the NRA quickly stumbled. The new governor of New York, Alonzo Cornell, had no interest in its marksmanship venture. State funding dried up, and the NRA had to close down Creedmoor and deed it back to the state. It took its nascent shooting competitions across state lines to New Jersey.

The Spanish-American War in 1898 revived the national interest in marksmanship and helped resurrect the NRA. At the urging of President Teddy Roosevelt, a gun enthusiast, Congress created the National Board for the Promotion of Rifle Practice as part of the Militia Act of 1903. Among its first acts, the board authorized the sale of surplus military weapons and ammunition to gun clubs sponsored by the NRA. The Army in 1910 started to donate arms and ammunition to the NRA. Congress even appropriated federal subsidies to help the NRA set up local shooting clubs across the country.

Even with all these government incentives, the NRA grew slowly. It had about 3,500 members in 1921, but thanks to its affiliation with local sporting clubs across the country, it grew to 35,000 by 1934 and 50,000 by the start of World War II.

In its early days, the NRA concentrated on building membership, teaching marksmanship, and holding competitions rather than lobbying in Washington. In 1907 it moved its headquarters to the capital and began to influence legislation.

During Prohibition in the 1920s and 1930s, bloody gangland battles mesmerized the country. Criminal gangs brandished sawed-off shotguns and machine guns to control illegal liquor sales. During Al Capone's St. Valentine's Day massacre in 1929, men disguised as Chicago police killed seven rivals with machine guns. Meanwhile, Bonnie and Clyde's bullet-laden bank heists riveted the nation.

The gangster violence and an assassination attempt on President Franklin Roosevelt in 1933 moved Congress to pass the National Firearms Act the following year. The law taxed and regulated the sale of machine guns and sawed-off shotguns. Sensing a threat to gun ownership, the NRA created a legislative division and asked members from around the country to contact their congressmen to argue against any regulation of handguns.

In May of the following year, the NRA's *Rifleman* magazine warned that the bill's "viciousness lies in the opportunity for disarmament by subterfuge." It urged readers to send telegrams or special-delivery letters to lobby senators and congressmen against the new law.

In committee, the NRA succeeded in stripping controls of handguns from the legislation.

In 1938, Congress laid the foundation for laws that would prevent gun violence by giving the executive branch the power to license gun and ammunition makers as well as firearms dealers and importers. The new laws also empowered the government to regulate interstate firearms sales. And with the NRA's backing, Congress barred convicted felons from legally buying guns of any type. But the law was weak. Licensing fees for dealers were low. And because prosecutors had to prove that gun sellers knew the buyers were felons, the laws were hard to enforce.

Karl T. Frederick, president of the NRA at the time, testified in support of the bill before Congress. "I have never believed in the general practice of carrying weapons," declared Frederick, who had won a gold medal for marksmanship in the 1920 Olympics before becoming a lawyer. "I do not believe in the general promiscuous toting of guns. I think it should be sharply restricted and only under licenses."

Frederick's comments were meant to sound reasonable, but behind the scenes and in committees, the NRA was already busy using tactics to undermine any attempts to regulate firearms.

Even so, had I been alive in the years following World War II, I would have been happy to join the NRA.

Before the war, the NRA concentrated on firearms training and marksmanship. The government helped by continuing to donate surplus rifles and ammunition from the US military to gun clubs sponsored by the NRA. Returning veterans swelled NRA ranks, not because they were paranoid and interested in stockpiling weaponry, but because they were hunters and wanted to sharpen their skills. Seizing the opportunity, the NRA promoted itself as a hunting club, and veterans joined up—raising its membership to more than three hundred thousand in the decade after the war.

In the 1950s, the NRA built up its staff and presence in Washington, DC, but it still didn't focus on lobbying Congress. The motto on its new headquarters in downtown DC in 1957 was "Firearms Safety Education, Marksmanship Training, Shooting for Recreation."

When NRA officials traveled to Capitol Hill, they wanted to discuss hunting, firearms safety, and wildlife management.

And then came the 1960s, a tumultuous decade marked by assassinations and gun violence.

In 1964, Lee Harvey Oswald assassinated President Kennedy with an Italian carbine rifle he bought for $21.45 via a mail-order ad in the NRA's magazine *American Rifle*. Soon thereafter, Connecticut Senator Thomas Dodd introduced President Lyndon Johnson's bill to restrict mail-order sales of rifles and shotguns. His son, retired Connecticut Senator Chris Dodd, spoke with me about that legislation. According to Senator Dodd, his father's bill "was a commonsense solution to address a serious issue."

The NRA's reaction revealed internal divisions within the organization. Franklin Orth, the NRA's executive vice president, testified before Congress in 1964. "We do not think that any sane American, who calls himself an American, can object to placing into this bill the instrument which killed the president of the United States," he declared. Orth's comments seemed to support Dodd's legislation, but the NRA successfully defeated attempts to register and license guns. Both were centerpieces of President Johnson's efforts at passing gun legislation.

"Our citizens must get licenses to fish, to hunt, and to drive," Johnson said after JFK's assassination. "Certainly no less should be required for the possession of lethal weapons that have caused so much horror and heartbreak in this country."

The NRA rallied its membership—then at nine hundred thousand—to defeat LBJ's bill. NRA President Harold Glassen testified before Senator Dodd's subcommittee that the bill was designed to "eventually disarm the American public."

Johnson's legislation failed.

"Both Houses rejected LBJ's call for registration," Josh Sugarmann wrote in his 1992 book on the NRA, "due in large part to an NRA mail blitz."

In April 1968, escaped convict James Earl Ray used a

30-06 Remington deer rifle to kill Martin Luther King Jr. on a balcony of the Lorraine Motel in Memphis. Ray bought the rifle under an assumed name. Two months later, Palestinian Sirhan Sirhan shot Senator Robert F. Kennedy dead with a .22 caliber target pistol in the kitchen of a Los Angeles hotel after a presidential-primary victory celebration.

The assassinations thrust a nation into mourning over beloved leaders killed by guns. Then urban riots in the late 1960s put gun legislation front and center in Washington and in statehouses around the country, especially in California, where Governor Ronald Reagan was making his mark.

Here's what Gabby and I unearthed about Reagan and gun legislation: in 1967, when Republicans in the California legislature came out in support of a law that would ban carrying a weapon in any city in the state, Reagan told reporters, "There's no reason why on the street today a citizen should be carrying loaded weapons." He called guns "a ridiculous way to solve problems that have to be solved among people of goodwill."

Reagan was by no means alone in his moderate views on guns. Much of the nation felt uneasy about the growing waves of gun violence, and toward the end of the decade Congress passed the Gun Control Act of 1968—but not without acrimonious opposition along the way. The NRA worked to weaken the bill in committee. On the Senate floor, Senator Thomas Dodd accused the NRA of "blackmail, intimidation, and unscrupulous propaganda." In its final form, the bill banned the interstate shipment of firearms and ammunition to private individuals. It prohibited the sale of guns to minors, convicted felons, drug addicts, and mental incompetents. It banned the mail-order sale of firearms, like the one used to kill President Kennedy.

Importing foreign-made weapons was now illegal. The law also increased penalties for people convicted of using a gun in the commission of a crime covered by federal law.

The NRA generally supported the final bill, but one component of the legislation would create a schism among its members. Under the new law, licensed firearms dealers were required to record the details of each gun transaction. These "yellow sheets" were open to inspection by federal agents in the Bureau of Alcohol, Tobacco and Firearms (ATF), a new division of the Treasury Department.

Some in the NRA leadership welcomed the new rules, believing they would help keep guns out of the hands of felons, fugitives, and the mentally unbalanced while giving law-abiding citizens a clear path to gun ownership. But a growing number of NRA leaders began to bristle at any attempt to pass commonsense gun laws. They were especially concerned about the ATF, a federal agency focused on firearms.

Then, in the mid-1970s, these two NRA factions went to war.

*   *   *

Maxwell Rich was my kind of NRA leader. A retired major general, Rich was skeptical of lobbying Congress to beat back moderate gun-violence-prevention policies. He was satisfied with the 1968 Gun Control Act. Sick of Washington and its overheated conflicts, Rich and his allies on the NRA board wanted to return the association to its roots in shooting sports and education. They were dubbed the Old Guard.

In 1976, Rich unveiled a plan to sell the NRA's national headquarters on Sixteenth Street, seven blocks from the White House, and move the headquarters to Colorado

Springs, Colorado. Rather than battle to protect "threatened" Second Amendment rights, Rich and company wanted to trade political activism for a less complicated NRA rooted in conservation issues, gun-safety training, and marksmanship.

Congressman John Dingell—who is now the longest-serving member of Congress and one of the colleagues Gabby had always admired the most—had a different plan. The Michigan Democrat was a die-hard gun-rights advocate and NRA member. He believed his colleagues in Congress and in statehouses across the country were on a mission to further regulate guns. He convinced the NRA board to establish a formal lobbying arm, the Institute for Legislative Action.

Under its first executive director, Harlon Bronson Carter, the ILA became a powerful lobbying force. With his folksy, South Texas drawl, people could get the sense that Carter was a harmless good ol' boy. He was stocky and shaved his head. He'd been associated with the NRA board throughout a long career in federal law enforcement, starting with the Border Patrol. But his looks belied his savvy. Carter was smart, experienced, and dedicated to protecting Second Amendment rights as he saw them.

As we learned about Harlon Carter, Gabby and I began to think of him as the godfather of the extreme gun-rights faction, a group that sees government as a dark force bent on disarming the citizenry. Carter would publicly compare any attempt at regulating guns to Nazi Germany's laws to keep guns from citizens.

* * *

Maxwell Rich and the Old Guard would need funds for their move to Colorado. To reduce expenses, they started by cutting the NRA staff by eighty in November 1976, targeting in particular those opposed to the move. In NRA lore, it's called the "Weekend Massacre."

Harlon Carter resigned before he was fired. But Carter didn't disappear; he simply went rogue. He sought out NRA members in gun clubs and associations around the country who shared his fear that Second Amendment rights were in jeopardy and his conviction that the Old Guard was not in the least interested in protecting them.

Carter found a kindred spirit in Neal Knox. A fellow Texan, Knox started off as a journalist for small-town newspapers but found his true calling in writing about guns and gun rights in *Gun Week* and then *Rifle* magazine. Like Carter, Knox believed the government had no right to pass any law concerning guns. None whatsoever. He wanted to roll back gun laws all the way to the 1934 law that regulated machine guns. Try this for a conspiracy theory: Knox wondered if the assassinations of Martin Luther King and Bobby Kennedy were concocted as part of a plot to strengthen regulations of guns. Today, there are people who believe that the Newtown shooting was staged for the same reason.

In 1977, Carter and Knox masterminded a plot to take over the NRA. At the association's annual convention in Cincinnati, they flooded the floor with like-minded members from around the country, tightly organized into a subversive group that called itself the Federation of the NRA. Under NRA bylaws, the board had to consider any motion from a member from the floor.

As Maxwell Rich and the Old Guard tried to maintain control of the convention and cement their plan to move the association to Colorado, Carter and Knox unleashed a campaign of disruption. Their allies wore orange hats and communicated by walkie-talkies. Making motions from the floor and voting in lockstep, the rebellion forced a vote to replace the board of directors. They moved to change the group's bylaws to make opposing any attempt to pass laws that would prevent gun violence central to the NRA's mission. They resurrected the Institute for Legislative Action, Harlon Carter's defunct lobbying arm.

The session in a hot and clammy hall lasted far into the night. Just before dawn broke, Maxwell Rich and the Old Guard found themselves pushed to the sidelines. Harlon Carter emerged as the NRA's new executive vice president, with Neal Knox by his side.

The NRA stayed in Washington, DC. Carter installed a new motto over the entrance to the association's headquarters: "The Right of the People to Keep and Bear Arms Shall Not Be Infringed."

*　*　*

The decade following the so-called Revolt at Cincinnati in 1977 became the NRA's Golden Age. The NRA finally had a cause that it could use to grow its ranks. In short order, its membership went from nine hundred thousand to three million. Its budget doubled. It was well on its way to becoming the political and lobbying powerhouse it is today.

One of Neal Knox's first moves was to reestablish and strengthen the NRA's lobbying arm. One of his first hires was Wayne LaPierre, a smart young Democratic Party legislative aide from Roanoke, Virginia. LaPierre was a rumpled, frenetic fellow more interested in the minutiae of the *Congressional Record* than the velocity of a .225 caliber round. But LaPierre would embark on a relentless quest to become an executive of the NRA, eclipsing both Harlon Carter and Neal Knox.

Born in upstate New York, LaPierre was an odd fit inside the

NRA. He was neither a hunter nor a marksman and seemed to have little interest in firearms. He wasn't "gunny enough." The joke around the NRA was that if you went duck hunting with Wayne, you were in more danger than the ducks.

LaPierre—with his undergraduate degree in education from a private liberal arts college and his master's degree in government from Boston College—was the picture of the highly educated elitist that his organization made so much money mocking. Before coming to the NRA in 1978, LaPierre had worked as a statehouse staffer in Richmond. For the NRA, he first oversaw lobbying and legislative affairs in the northeast states. By 1982, he had risen to become director of the NRA's federal lobbying division in Washington.

Ricochet author Richard Feldman first met LaPierre in the early 1980s, when both were working in the NRA's lobbying division.

"His handshake was weak," Feldman wrote. "He avoided our eyes, and his expression was almost furtive."

Feldman would later chalk up LaPierre's demeanor to shyness. He also recognized LaPierre's prowess as a "true politics junkie"—and that ability, more than any personal magnetism, propelled LaPierre to leadership within the NRA.

In his days running the NRA's lobbying division, LaPierre worked closely with James Jay Baker. The two made a perfect team: LaPierre was the studious inside operator, counting votes and writing legislative language; Baker fit the profile of a swashbuckling Washington player, perfectly suited to play the NRA's outside guy on Capitol Hill. He dressed in fine suits, sported wavy hair and a full mustache, and adored big game hunting.

LaPierre and Baker oversaw the NRA's intense lobbying drive that resulted in the 1986 legislative amendments that essentially gutted the Gun Control Act of 1968. Among other changes, the Firearms Owners Protection Act of 1986 made it easier for people to sell guns without a license, as long as they were not in the regular business of dealing firearms. The bill essentially created the loophole that has allowed the sale of weapons at gun shows and over the Internet, without the need for the buyer to pass a background check.

By 1991, Wayne LaPierre had grown from a bookish political strategist to a more polished operator both outside and inside the NRA. He started to dress and act more like his ally, James Baker. He avoided conflict, but he turned his Institute for Legislative Action, which he had run since 1986, into the source of the NRA's power.

At the NRA's 1991 annual meeting in San Antonio, the group elected forty-one-year-old Wayne LaPierre executive vice president, one of the organization's top jobs. He was in charge of the NRA's seventy-six-member board of directors and the group's policy, lobbying, and overall operations.

"Critics in the media have referred to me as a 'hardliner,'" LaPierre wrote in his first column to the membership as the leader, "probably not realizing that I accept their words as a compliment."

But even then, LaPierre was less of a hardliner than he would become. By the time the NRA faced its greatest public-relations crisis almost a quarter of a century later, LaPierre was an old hand at riling up his followers. He had no doubt learned that the more outrageous his predictions were, the more guns would fly off the shelves, the more money his organization would rake in, and the more power he would amass.

CHAPTER SIX

NEWTOWN

A dam Lanza lived in Newtown, Connecticut, with his mother, Nancy. At twenty, he was, by most accounts, isolated and disturbed, a virtual shut-in whose psychiatric problems had surfaced in early childhood. He had received all sorts of professional evaluations and diagnoses—sensory integration disorder, Asperger's syndrome—and had been prescribed a range of medications over the years, but his behavior only got more erratic and disturbed as he grew older.

Nancy Lanza, by contrast, was sociable and well liked, though the strain of being a single parent caring for an emotionally troubled son (who, despite never leaving the house, changed clothes several times a day and would only communicate with his mother by e-mail) had increased in recent years. She indulged her son's every whim, including his interest in firearms.

On the morning of December 14, 2012, Adam Lanza entered his mother's bedroom and shot her four times in bed. He took three guns from the basement where Nancy stored her collection: a Bushmaster AR-15 assault rifle and two semiautomatic pistols. Then, wearing black military fatigues and an olive-green utility vest stuffed with high-capacity magazines, he drove across the bucolic Connecticut town to Sandy Hook Elementary School.

It was an expectant, pre-holiday morning at the school. Teachers were starting their lessons for the approximately seven hundred students. Principal Dawn Hochsprung was meeting with her staff. Over the sound of morning announcements, students and teachers heard the pop-pop-pop of gunshots. Adam Lanza had blasted his way through the school's glass security doors and stormed into the front hallway.

Hochsprung, school psychologist Mary Sherlach, and teacher Natalie Hammond were in the central office when they heard the shots and went into the hallway to investigate.

"Shooter!" one cried. "Stay put."

Lanza opened fire with the AR-15. He killed Hochsprung and Sherlach and wounded Hammond. Hearing the gunfire, teachers started herding students into bathrooms and closets. Lanza walked toward two classrooms. He shot a substitute teacher and all fourteen students in one room. He burst into the next classroom and shot teacher Victoria Soto and six students.

As police arrived, Lanza pulled out a pistol and shot himself in the head. In fewer than five minutes, he had killed twenty children—ages six and seven—and six adults.

* * *

"Enough."

That was one of Gabby's first words to me after we learned the nightmarish details of the Newtown massacre. Her simple verdict grounded me and focused all around her.

The Aurora shooting in July 2012 had shocked us: the

shooter had taken a dozen lives and wounded fifty-eight more—people who just wanted to see a movie. We saw parallels to Tucson. During our vacation that summer in 2012, we constantly talked about broader gun-violence problems in our country, and what we might do to prevent another shooting rampage.

Newtown jarred us past good intentions and wishful thinking. Newtown moved us from words to action.

In early January 2013, while our nation was still in mourning over Newtown, we began building an organization that would work to curb the epidemic of gun violence that has spread even to the quietest corners of America. We wanted to accomplish several major goals: inspire a national dialogue about gun violence that's based on facts and not fear; raise enough money to help level the playing field with the gun lobby so that politicians can start voting with their consciences—and their constituents' wills—again; and support some commonsense measures that would keep guns out of the hands of the wrong people.

This was a massive undertaking, and we knew we couldn't do it alone. Starting from scratch, we needed staff, supporters, and contributors. We began contacting Gabby's friends, allies, and colleagues to see if they could envision her in this new role. As a state legislator and congresswoman, Gabby had never been laser-focused on a single issue. She'd always devoted her energies to a broad array of interests—solar energy, border security, veteran care—so it was by no means a given that she'd focus on gun laws. But as soon as we presented our plans to try and prevent the next mass murder, Gabby's supporters at home and in Congress rallied around us.

I spent hours talking on the phone and days meeting face-to-face with potential donors. Once I felt we could raise some serious funds, we convinced Pia Carusone, Gabby's former chief of staff, to join our new venture as executive director. Pia had managed Gabby's congressional office from the shooting until her resignation. When Gabby stepped down, Pia had taken on a high-profile job as Assistant Secretary of the Department of Homeland Security for Public Affairs, but we had stayed close.

We also brought on Peter Ambler and Hayley Zachary. Peter had been Gabby's legislative director; he now agreed to be our chief strategist and oversee our lobbying operation. Hayley had worked on Gabby's political campaigns as her finance director. She had moved to Tucson in January 2012 to work for Ron Barber, who was elected that June to succeed Gabby in the House. Hayley agreed to run our fundraising team.

The legal and regulatory framework came together relatively quickly, thanks to Pia and Hayley, who worked with our lawyers to establish our political action committees.

Next we needed a name.

In Congress, Gabby was a problem solver. She was a moderate who always tried to reach consensus on policies she thought were both reasonable and responsible. We tossed names back and forth. We knew what the name should *not* contain: no *guns*, no *rifles*, no *control*, no *violence*. We weren't *against* anything; we simply wanted to bring people together to solve real problems.

After New Year's Day, in recognition of Gabby's hallmark values, we named our organization Americans for Responsible Solutions.

* * *

Just three weeks after Newtown, we were approaching the second anniversary of the Tucson shooting. We had started to raise funds. We had a team in place and a name for our new organization. We arranged to launch Americans for Responsible Solutions on January 8, during an exclusive interview with ABC's Diane Sawyer. We flew to New York after New Year's to prepare and visit with a few potential supporters.

At the same time, the families of the children and adults killed at the Sandy Hook Elementary School invited us to visit them in Newtown. They sought solace from Gabby. Many of the parents wanted to see her, talk to her, and share their grief with a woman who had lived through a massacre. Some of the Newtown families contacted us and offered to host the meeting.

On Friday, January 4, we drove northeast from Manhattan to Connecticut. During the ninety-minute drive, the car was relatively quiet. We had no idea what to expect. We were still trying to comprehend the facts emerging from that horrible day at Sandy Hook Elementary.

Gabby and I knew how to provide comfort for people in pain. We had experienced firsthand the wreckage left in the wake of a mass shooting: the shock, the disbelief, the emptiness, the heartbreak, the constant struggle to pick up the pieces and resume living a normal life. But for us and for the entire nation, Newtown felt different. Lanza shot little children in their classrooms. Most of us think of our children's schools as a sacred, safe place. Lanza had violated that sense of innocence and security with bursts of bullets from a weapon that belongs in the hands of the military or the police, or at the very least an incredibly responsible, mentally stable gun owner. It was a bridge too far.

"How can Americans accept a future," I asked Gabby and

111

the staff driving up with us, "where a young man with a long history of severe psychological problems could walk into a public school and open fire on young children like that?"

Visiting families in Sandy Hook would mark a new moment of trauma and pain for Gabby, one that she had missed after the Tucson shooting. In its immediate aftermath, she was recovering from a wound most thought would have killed her. As the rest of us spoke with bereaved families and attended funerals, Gabby was in surgery and rehab. It would be months before she could comprehend the human toll, share the loss, and begin to mourn.

In Newtown, she would have to confront raw, emotional wounds for the first time.

* * *

We arrived in Newtown just after noon. The ground was still covered from a recent snowfall and houses and streets were still adorned with Christmas decorations. It looked peaceful and idyllic.

Just off the highway, Gabby pointed out a pond where kids were playing hockey. We drove past classic New England homes with white clapboard siding, slate roofs, and white picket fences strung with lights.

"Looks like the perfect place to raise children," I said.

"Safe," Gabby responded. "So beautiful."

Some members of the national media were still camped out in Newtown, but we had not announced our visit. We had no interest in turning a private moment into a media circus. We slipped through downtown and pulled in front of the town hall. School superintendent Janet Robinson happened to be walking out. She took one look at Gabby and started to cry.

112

"We're so glad you came," she said. "Thank you."

Gabby hugged her.

Pat Llodra, Newtown's first selectman—the equivalent of the mayor—had asked to meet with us for a few minutes. She had invited US Senator Richard Blumenthal and Lieutenant Governor Nancy Wyman in for a private welcome. (The state's other US Senator, Chris Murphy, was being sworn in that morning.)

"We have to do something about these mass shootings," Llodra said.

"Gabby and I hope to help," I said. "There are things we think we can do."

We described our goals of building a national network of responsible gun owners to balance the political power in Washington and around the country. We talked about taking our case to Congress and drawing attention to gun laws that need to be strengthened so that the next Newtown might be averted.

Senator Blumenthal asked us to stay in touch and promised his support.

During our short meeting, word had gotten out that we were in town. A few reporters saw us leave the town hall. We were heading to visit Sandy Hook families, but the journalists kept their distance. We took the quick ride in silence. The landscape became hilly out of the village. Soon we arrived in the neighborhood around the Sandy Hook school, a scenic community of large homes.

Sandy Hook parents Tim and Melissa Makris had opened up their home for the gathering. He pointed out that Nancy and Adam Lanza had lived around the corner. We pulled into the driveway and entered through the basement playroom. Kids playing computer games barely noticed us. We passed through the kitchen, where parents had set out apple cider along with trays of crackers and cheese and some cookies. The Makris's living room was filled with the parents of some of the children killed in their classrooms as well as family members of some of the teachers who lost their lives.

Gabby visited and touched everyone. She has a way of creating a safe, comforting place. She doesn't need to talk much to communicate her love and understanding. She listened, empathized, and silently offered her sympathies.

The first person we saw was Natalie Hammond, the Sandy Hook teacher who had been standing with the principal and school psychologist in the hallway when Adam Lanza entered the school. Now she was seated in a chair next to the Christmas tree. Her foot, hand, and side were bandaged up. She wasn't even sure how many times she had been shot. She got up on her crutches, came over, and told us how lucky she was to be alive.

"Me, too," Gabby said, and gave her a very gentle hug.

A mother came over and showed us a photo of her daughter on her iPhone, and I just about lost it.

One couple after another came over to spend time with Gabby. Every single one of the bereaved parents brought pictures—on phones, in print, on cameras—of their beautiful children who had died that day. Lynn and Chris McDonnell presented us a magnet with a photo of their seven-year-old daughter, Grace. It would find a home in our kitchen in Tucson. The family of Victoria Soto, a young teacher shot and killed at the school, told us how much she had loved her job.

"We are still so shocked this could happen," one family member said, "especially at a school."

Gabby didn't have to speak. She stood with the families for an hour and a half. She listened, comforted them, hugged them. I talked with every parent. It is so difficult to find the right words for someone who has lost a child. Nothing we could say or do could ever bring their kid back. Sharing their mourning and offering physical comfort helped more than conversation.

After consoling every family, tearing up at every picture of innocent children who would never reach adulthood, Gabby became overwhelmed by the horror of the tragedy that had brought us there that day. She walked slowly over to an empty ottoman and lowered herself down onto it.

With her head in her one good hand, she said, "So awful. Enough."

*　　*　　*

Gabby and I assured the families we met at Sandy Hook that we were going to do something.

Visiting with them, hearing their tales of love and loss, had solidified our resolve. Sure, we had doubts. We faced the risk of taking on powerful Washington interest groups. We wondered if we could raise enough funds. People on both sides of this issue have very extreme views. Was there a personal risk to us and our family? Gabby and I were venturing into unexplored territory.

Our visit to Newtown eased most of those doubts and strengthened our resolve. Gabby's recovery had reached the point where she could take an active, more public role—but was I ready? I had never imagined that this kid from Jersey would explore space. I certainly could not have conceived a future where Gabby and I could become the faces of a national movement. But when the moment came, I knew we had no choice but to do our part.

On January 8, 2013—two years to the day after the bullet

tore through Gabby's brain—we officially launched Americans for Responsible Solutions.

"We have experienced too much death and hurt to remain idle," Gabby's op-ed in that day's *USA Today* declared. "Our response to the Newtown massacre must consist of more than regret, sorrow and condolence. The children of Sandy Hook Elementary School and all the victims of gun violence deserve fellow citizens and leaders who have the will to prevent gun violence in the future."

That morning our website went live on the Internet.

In the evening Diane Sawyer interviewed us on ABC's evening news. She began with a statistic: since the Tucson shooting, an estimated fifty-seven thousand adults and five thousand children had been killed by guns in the United States, including the twenty kids at Sandy Hook. "How do we get to the point where eighty-five percent of the children in the world that are killed with guns are killed in the United States?" I asked. "That is a sobering statistic."

"So that's what changed for you," Sawyer said.

"Yes," Gabby responded.

My left hand was on the arm of the chair. Gabby reached over with her good left hand and held mine.

Sawyer asked us about our hope that gun owners would join us to lead the movement for more sensible laws.

"You have a gun," she said.

"A Glock," Gabby said.

"Gabby and I are both gun owners," I responded. "We are strong supporters of the Second Amendment. I think most gun owners are in the same camp with us."

Plenty of my friends own firearms. They shoot, they hunt. I talk to gun owners all the time. Almost all of them firmly believe that a background check should be required before anyone buys a gun, that we should do whatever is possible to keep criminals from acquiring guns. In all my years of buying and using guns, I have never encountered a single gun owner who thinks that people afflicted with mental illness should have access to firearms. Believe it or not, many gun owners also believe there should be restrictions on magazine size and some laws pertaining specifically to access to assault weapons.

Sawyer said our new group sought to work with Congress to change laws concerning background checks and magazine sizes. I mentioned I had recently gone through a background check to buy a gun.

"Why can't we make it more difficult for criminals and the mentally ill to get guns?" I asked.

Sawyer responded with the NRA's view that people would simply try to obtain guns illegally if they wanted to avoid background checks.

"I don't agree with that," I said. "The gun lobby even opposes a gun purchaser being checked against a terrorist watch list." I held out my hands and asked: "Doesn't that seem like a commonsense thing to do?"

What about the argument, she posed, that the only thing that stops a bad guy with a gun is a good guy with a gun? If there had been someone with a gun in that parking lot with Jared Loughner—

"There was," I interrupted. "There was somebody with a gun other than Jared Loughner." I explained that he had thought about using it but kept it in his pocket. A good guy with a gun "nearly shot the man who took down Jared Loughner," I said, echoing Joe Zamudio's words from the day of the Tucson shooting.

And there was absolutely no proof that "good guys with

guns" made any difference in other shootings, either. A recent investigation found that *not one* of the sixty-two mass shootings over the last thirty years has been stopped by good guys with guns—even when they've tried. At Columbine, armed guards traded fire with Dylan Klebold and Eric Harris. And late last year, shooter Aaron Alexis dispossessed an armed guard of his gun at the Washington Navy Yard, disproving one of the NRA's favorite theories yet again.

Long before this latest tragic shooting, Gabby and I had decided that the time had come to start countering the NRA's fantasies with some hard facts.

* * *

In addition to outlining what we hoped to accomplish and serving as an information resource, the Americans for Responsible Solutions website gave supporters the opportunity to contribute. We needed about $1 million to set up our organization, hire staff, rent space, file paperwork to establish our PACs, build a website, and lay the groundwork for a lasting organization. Beyond that, our goal of raising enough money to go toe-to-toe with the gun lobby would require more than $20 million each election cycle.

Hayley Zachary and I were wondering about our website's success the day before the launch. She had been with us in New York and Newtown.

"Hayley," I asked, "how much do you think we will raise tomorrow?"

"A few thousand dollars," she guessed.

"I hope we do much better," I said.

We did. At the end of our first day people had contributed $190,000, mostly in five-to-ten-dollar donations. Added to the funds I had raised before and during the holidays and our visit to New York, we had brought in more than $1.5 million.

That was nowhere near enough to match the gun lobby's war chest, but it was certainly an impressive start.

CHAPTER SEVEN

HOW THE NRA
CONTROLS CONGRESS

A week after the slaughter of children and adults at Sandy Hook Elementary School, Wayne LaPierre delivered his solution. The NRA wanted "armed security" in every school and would later advocate arming principals and teachers as well.

After briefly mourning the twenty children, the NRA's executive vice president doubled down on the good-guy-with-a-gun theory and blasted the media in a trademark, wild-eyed screed.

"Rather than face their own moral failings," LaPierre announced at the hotly anticipated press conference in Washington, DC, "the media demonize lawful gun owners, amplify their cries for more gun laws, and fill the national debate with misinformation and dishonest thinking that only delay meaningful action and all but guarantee that the next atrocity is only a news cycle away." When politicians pass laws for gun-free school zones, La Pierre said, they're signaling to "every insane killer in America that schools are the safest place to inflict maximum mayhem with minimum risk"—a phrase typical of the fearmongering that LaPierre has elevated into an art form over the years.

And yet just over a decade earlier, in the wake of the Columbine school shooting, LaPierre *supported* gun-free school zones. He said at the time, "We believe in absolutely gun-free, zero-tolerance, totally safe schools. That means no guns in America's schools, period . . . with the rare exception of law enforcement officers or trained security personnel."

But, as with so much else at the NRA, LaPierre had embraced more extreme views with every passing year, even (or especially) as the impact of gun violence on our society became more prominent. As his reversal on gun-free schools showed, he was a chronic flip-flopper. He'd once supported waiting periods and universal background checks and later vehemently opposed both measures.

A week after Newtown, LaPierre had changed his tune once again to blame the shooting on gun-control measures, rather than the shooter himself: "When it comes to our most beloved, innocent, and vulnerable members of the American family, our children, we as a society leave them every day utterly defenseless, and the monsters and the predators of the world know it, and exploit it," LaPierre said.

LaPierre then called on Congress "to act immediately, to appropriate whatever is necessary to put armed police officers in every school—and do it now, to make sure that blanket of safety is in place when our children return to school in January." After all, as he had insisted repeatedly over the years, "The only thing that stops a bad guy with a gun is a good guy with a gun." I thought again of Joe Zamudio, a "good guy" with the best of intentions who had come very close to shooting the man who had wrestled the gun away from Jared Loughner, and shivered.

The *New York Daily News* wrote that to the NRA, "the only answer to death by guns is to flood the country with more guns and stand ready for the shootout."

"Mendacious, delusional, almost deranged rant" is how the *New York Times* described LaPierre's remedy.

But here's the thing about LaPierre's "rant": it wasn't delusional or deranged at all. It was perfectly calculated, and right on target. Why do you think the normally in-your-face NRA had been silent for an entire week after the school shootings? Was it because its members were trying to be "respectably silent," as LaPierre claimed, of the tragedy? Or was it because they'd been doing their research and carefully calibrating their reaction to win them the best possible (and most profitable) advantage?

The approach the NRA settled on was perfectly reflected in the press conference LaPierre held that day. Sure, his "School Shield Program" might turn off mainstream, middle-of-the-road Americans—but so what? The mainstream wasn't the NRA's target audience. LaPierre's speech was directed at the fringe, and his alarmist message hit the bull's-eye. Want to protect yourself from the "monsters and the predators" roaming through the hallways of your children's school? Better buy more guns. Gun sales went through the roof in the weeks after Newtown, and the NRA profited in the process.

In the wake of Newtown, the NRA chose to take a short-term hit in the news media for the long-term gain of riling up the most scared elements of our society. Rather than appeal to the best instincts in all of us, why not feed the basest impulses of some? The organization had cashed in on the effectiveness of this tactic for years.

*   *   *

123

Wayne LaPierre is a canny survivor who's been the leader and the voice of the NRA since 1991. In that time, he has become an extremely talented performer who can play to his audience brilliantly: he might not buy his own overblown rhetoric, but he seemed to have learned from long experience that fear was the best route to selling guns. He also knew that the more guns people bought, the more money the NRA would collect.

LaPierre also knew exactly how his words would reverberate on Capitol Hill.

President Barack Obama flew to Newtown days after Adam Lanza's rampage. He said December 14 was the toughest day of his presidency, comforted the families who had lost loved ones, and vowed to reform the nation's gun laws. But many in Congress were hesitant. True, some senators and members of Congress mourned with the Newtown families, but precious few—whether Republican or Democrat—broached the subject of legislation that might prevent future mass murders or dared to mention the daily toll that gun violence takes on our country. Were they too stunned to speak? Nope. When it came to guns, the NRA literally controlled when many lawmakers opened their mouths, what they said, and how they voted.

How could this be? How did it come to pass that a nation based on a representative democracy wound up with legislators who represent one interest group against the wishes and welfare of the majority of citizens?

We put the question to Bill Clinton. Gabby and I had run into the former president in New York at a performance of *Ann*, a play about legendary former Texas governor Ann Richards. Clinton had pushed through the assault-weapons ban in 1994, the nation's last significant gun law.

"What did it take?" Gabby asked.

"It takes moral courage," Clinton responded. "Sometimes people have to stand up and do the right thing. They have to be willing to risk a vote for the greater good, rather than their political future."

But that was more generalization than history lesson.

"Can you explain the politics?" I asked.

Clinton gave us a short course on how he'd engineered the assault-weapons law through Congress. He described a four-year struggle that succeeded in part because he enlisted the help of cabinet members, especially Treasury Secretary Lloyd Bentsen, a Texan and gun owner. He talked about personally lobbying conservative House members, such as Illinois Republican Henry Hyde. He mentioned Tom Foley and Jack Brooks, brave congressmen who voted their conscience against the NRA and may have just lost their seats for it.

Clinton's insights helped guide us. But Gabby and I also needed to know how the NRA built its political machine, which many called the most powerful interest group in the nation. If we understood how it worked, maybe we could build a more effective counterpart.

J. Warren Cassidy, after he served as NRA executive vice president in the 1980s, often said, "You would get a far better understanding if you approached us as if you were approaching one of the great religions of the world."

Wow. How did a rifle club become a religion?

*　*　*

Tom Foley didn't know what hit him. Jack Brooks didn't, either. Both veteran lawmakers were staunch supporters of gun rights and the NRA, but when they dared to go against

125

the NRA one time on a crucial assault-weapons-ban vote, they paid a steep price.

Gabby would have adored Foley. He was a tall, lean, white-haired Democrat from Washington State. He had served thirty years in Congress and had risen to Speaker of the House in 1989. He was an ardent NRA supporter. A gentle, stately gentleman, he was well loved by all, so he thought.

Jack Brooks, a salty Democrat from Texas, would have been a Gabby favorite, too. In his forty-four years in Congress, he helped write the Civil Rights Act of 1964 and the Voting Rights Act of 1965. As chairman of the Judiciary Committee, he played a key role in the impeachment proceedings against Richard Nixon. Like Foley, Brooks was a lifetime NRA supporter.

Neither Foley nor Brooks could have foreseen the role guns would play in their reelection battles.

For most of the 1970s and '80s, guns were not at the forefront of the minds of Americans or their representatives in Washington, DC. The National Rifle Association spent those decades quietly and successfully building its membership, fattening its coffers, and beating back any reasonable gun legislation. It helped write and push through the 1986 Firearms Owners Protection Act that loosened many of the restrictions in the 1968 gun legislation.

Two massacres put guns back in the news.

In January 1989, Patrick Purdy, a twenty-four-year-old drifter, brought an AK-47 assault rifle to Cleveland Elementary School in Stockton, California. He had fitted it with a "drum" magazine that held seventy-five bullets. Purdy arrived at the school shortly before noon. He opened fire in the schoolyard, killing five students and wounding thirty-three others. After firing 105 rounds, Purdy killed himself with a pistol. It was a chilling precursor to Sandy Hook.

Two years later, George Hennard crashed his Ford Ranger pickup through the window of Luby's cafeteria in Killeen, Texas, a small town northwest of Houston and home of Fort Hood. He drew a pair of semiautomatic pistols and started shooting patrons. He shot fifty and killed twenty-three. Hennard was a disgruntled unemployed Merchant Mariner. When police showed up, he hid in a bathroom and shot himself in the head.

In the aftermath of these two shootings, Americans, already fearful of rising crime rates, started to ask: do civilians need weapons capable of such slaughter? A 1993 CNN/ *USA Today*/Gallup poll counted 77 percent of Americans supporting a ban on the manufacture, sale, and possession of what were known as semiautomatic assault weapons.

So-called assault rifles—and even the name would become controversial in the years to come—differ from other weapons in a few significant ways. Designed for military use, they are light and have relatively short barrels. Almost all can accept high-capacity, detachable magazines that can hold twenty, thirty, or up to one hundred rounds of ammunition. But like standard semiautomatic pistols and rifles, they fire a round only each time you pull the trigger, rather than firing continuously like a machine gun.

Most of these guns have pistol grips. They often have collapsible or folding stocks and flash suppressors attached to the barrel's end that reduce the muzzle flash, to help shield the shooter's position. Some have "lugs" to accept a bayonet. It is features like this that make the gun useful in combat. There's a reason you don't go to war with a hunting rifle.

They often have a rugged combat-inspired look, which is

the intent of the manufacturer: to appeal to those gun hobby-ists who shop at the army-navy store and speak in acronyms but have never actually considered serving in the military. This wannabe-military crowd had become an increasingly prominent force in American life, and people were starting to take notice.

*　*　*

Reacting to public outrage about the Stockton massacre, President George H. W. Bush banned the import of certain assault rifles in 1989. Bush was a hunter and lifetime NRA member, but that one act put him on the gun group's enemy list. Some called for him to be expelled. President Clinton, who was unassociated with and unafraid of the NRA, broad-ened the import ban in 1993 and 1998.

Congress began taking up complete bans on assault weap-ons in 1989, but the NRA successfully stripped them out of every piece of legislation—until 1993, when the Senate passed a bill sponsored by California Senator Dianne Fein-stein to ban the manufacture of nineteen assault weapons.

The legislation bounced back and forth between the Senate and House. Amid much horse-trading, the assault-weapons ban survived as part of an omnibus criminal justice bill. The $30 billion package included financing for one hun-dred thousand new police officers, an expansion of the fed-eral death penalty, and funds for crime-prevention programs.

Bill Clinton sold the bill as anticrime rather than antigun, and it was. At every opportunity, he surrounded himself with police officers. By this time, the NRA had lost any sympathy or support from police. In the 1980s the organization fought tooth and nail against stopping the sale of Teflon-coated "cop-killer bullets." These bullets were originally designed for law-enforcement use to pierce metal, but criminals could use them to shoot through a cop's Kevlar vest. Ever since, law enforcement had fought for gun-control measures that the NRA more and more reflexively opposed.

I remember my detective dad calling the NRA's support for cop-killer bullets "disappointing and dangerous."

The assault-weapons ban was a short section of an enormous bill. And it had an expiration date. It outlawed for ten years the manufacture, sale, and possession of nineteen assault weapons by name and many others that incorporated specific assault-weapon characteristics. It also specifically exempted 661 sporting rifles. It limited ammunition magazines to ones that could hold no more than ten bullets.

Meanwhile, the legislation made plenty of provisions to satisfy gun owners. It grandfathered in assault weapons that people already owned, and the bill was written in such a way that gun manufacturers could keep manufacturing the weapons—as long as they eliminated any two of the named assault-weapon characteristics, including bayonet mounts, pistol grips, or flash suppressors. Back in the mid-1990s, before the law went into effect, manufacturers ratcheted up production, and gun owners snapped up the weapons.

By this stage in the debate, even the term "assault weapon" had become a dirty word for the NRA, and it remains so today. As the organization argued, any weapon—a knife, a baseball bat—can be an assault weapon if used to assault someone. That's true enough—but it's also true that some assault weapons are more dangerous than others. There's a reason we equip soldiers with fully automatic M16s instead of baseball bats.

Still, I also believed that the arbitrary parameters used to define the term "assault weapon"—many of which are cosmetic details that do little to alter the lethality of the weapon—missed the point. So what if your gun *looks* scary? Obviously, the AR-15's tough military appearance is a big reason for its popularity among the army-navy store shoppers. Because even though the AR-15 has a straight-out-of-*Rambo* look, it's also lightweight and incredibly easy to shoot, without much recoil. An AR-15 owner can project all the badass qualities of the military with none of the experience.

The appearance of a gun makes no difference; its lethality does. Instead of arguing over the accessories, why aren't we talking about what really matters, like magazine size? In a typical line of reasoning, the NRA claims that limiting the size of a magazine simply means that a shooter will bring multiple mags and just reload, that the magazine size won't change the course of an event since a shooter can change the magazine in two seconds.

But history simply doesn't bear out that argument. Its logic (or lack of logic) implies that mass shootings are calm events overseen by stable individuals, when we all know that the opposite is true. In the chaos of a shooting, even the tiniest pause could be the difference between six people dead and sixty. In Tucson on that awful day, every single one of the thirty-three bullets in Loughner's magazine hit somebody. It was pausing to reload that brought the whole event to a halt. Gabby and I shudder to imagine how much worse the shooting could've turned out if Loughner's magazine had contained a hundred rounds. And we also think about who might still be alive if it had only contained ten.

* * *

The assault-weapons ban enraged the NRA, as did the Brady Bill that had passed the previous year.

In March 1981, John Hinckley Jr. attempted to assassinate Ronald Reagan. The president survived a bullet wound, but his press secretary, Jim Brady, took a bullet in the head and never fully recovered. His wife, Sarah Brady, became active in the gun-violence movement and leader of the Brady Center to Prevent Gun Violence, formerly known as Handgun Control, Inc., established in 1980.

Brady's group proposed a law that would require background checks for gun purchases nationwide and require a five-day waiting period for handguns. Congress took up the legislation in 1987; the Brady Bill finally passed in 1993.

For decades, the NRA had supported waiting periods. "A waiting period could help in reducing crimes of passion in preventing people with criminal records or dangerous mental illness from acquiring guns," an NRA pamphlet from the 1970s said. But by the early 1990s, the NRA had begun to travel further and further right on a number of issues, a drift that would become even more pronounced later: Remember how in 1999 LaPierre had supported gun-free school zones but later reversed his stance? That same year, he had expressed support for mandatory background checks for all gun sales, another middle-ground position he'd later reject.

So the NRA's earlier flip-flop on waiting periods came as no surprise to Gabby and me when we viewed it as part of the larger story. Remember, LaPierre had been hardening the NRA party line on all sorts of issues, and waiting periods were no exception. Despite the NRA's earlier openness to waiting periods as an effective measure for keeping guns out of the hands of the wrong people, by 1994 LaPierre was fighting the proposal as an infringement on constitutional rights. It was, in his view, "the first step toward more stringent 'gun control' measures" that would lead to complete disarmament.

Ronald Reagan, the first president to get the NRA's backing, was serving his final year when Congress took up the Brady Bill, and long out of office by the time it passed. But when the NRA bitterly fought the bill named for his friend and press secretary, the Gipper said in a 1991 speech: "You know that I'm a member of the NRA and my position on the right to bear arms is well-known, but I want you to know something else, and I am going to say it in clear, unmistakable language: I support the Brady Bill, and I urge Congress to enact it without further delay."

The NRA attempted to kill or water down the bill for seven years, but Congress finally passed the law in November 1993 during President Clinton's first term.

The NRA issued its verdict on the Brady Bill in *American Rifleman*: "When Bill Clinton signed the Brady Bill into law on November 30, a drop of blood dripped from the finger of the sovereign American citizen."

* * *

When it came to the assault-weapons ban, the NRA was even more determined to punish any lawmakers who strayed from its orthodoxy. Both Tom Foley and Jack Brooks had ended up voting for the final legislation because in the end, they believed it was the right thing to do—as Bill Clinton told us.

They weren't fully prepared for the backlash their votes would cause. The National Rifle Association vowed vengeance in the midterm elections of November 1994. In mailings and meetings, the NRA used the assault-weapons ban to raise money, attract members, and target every congressman who voted for the omnibus crime bill that included the ban.

The September 1994 cover of *American Rifleman* depicted

a shirtless politician with a yellow band down his back. The headline: YOU TRUSTED THEM WITH YOUR FREEDOM AND NOW . . . TOO MANY POLITICIANS SHOW THEIR STRIPES.

The October issue, with a state-by-state voter guide, ran a painting of Lady Liberty on the cover. The same politician was assaulting her from behind, but this time he wore a dark suit and tie. One hand covered her mouth, the other ripped off her robe. The cover said: STOP THE RAPE OF LIBERTY.

Inside the magazine, the voter's-guide headline read: IT'S PAYBACK TIME.

The NRA exacted revenge on Democrats who voted for the assault-weapons ban, even powerful members of Congress who had been stalwart gun-rights supporters for decades. The NRA spent $114,710 against Tom Foley's reelection in Washington State. Foley lost to newcomer George Nethercutt. It marked the first time a Speaker of the House had lost an election since 1862. While the changing demographics of Foley's district also played a major role in his defeat, the NRA had done its part, too.

In Texas, the NRA withdrew its support for Jack Brooks in his reelection bid, and Brooks lost to an unknown Republican. He was the longest-serving member of the House to lose an election.

But the NRA didn't always hit its mark.

In the 1994 election, in trying to defeat Senator Bob Kerrey of Nebraska, the NRA put Charlton Heston on TV to say: "You said you wouldn't vote for gun bans. But you went to Washington and voted for the first federal gun ban in American history." Even with Heston blasting away, the NRA failed to unseat Kerrey.

Still, in that pivotal election, Republicans gained fifty-four seats and took over the House for the first time since

1954. Of course, few political scientists would argue that the House went to the Republicans solely because the NRA wanted to knock off Democrats who voted for the assault-weapons ban. As in any election, many factors came into play: a more conservative electorate, the typical dissatisfaction we normally see with the president's party in a midterm election, a struggling health care–reform bill, and the zeal for change pushed by Newt Gingrich and his "Contract with America."

Gingrich's Contract conspicuously did not include a plank on guns—but still, it was no accident that as soon as he became the new Speaker, Gingrich promised no gun-violence legislation would pass the House. And Bill Clinton offered this (conveniently self-exonerating) verdict to the *Cleveland Plain Dealer*: "The NRA is the reason the Republicans control the House."

Inside its headquarters, NRA officials joked that their acronym stood for "Never Reelected Again."

*　*　*

After the 1994 midterms, members of Congress got the message loud and clear: cross the NRA and risk losing your job. For the next two decades, the National Rifle Association wielded power over gun laws, regulations, and as many congressional seats as possible.

It tallied every vote and assessed every comment by the 435 house members and 100 senators. It graded each congressman. The organization took a bare-knuckle approach to oppose any attempt at regulating guns, bullets, or firearm sales—by whatever means necessary.

Here's an example.

Eric Harris and Dylan Klebold were too young to buy

guns, so they asked Klebold's older friend Robyn Anderson to buy some for them at a gun show. She didn't have to undergo a background check because it was a "private sale." In April 1999, Harris and Klebold took the guns to Columbine High School in Littleton, Colorado, where they opened fire on students and teachers. They killed twelve students and one teacher and wounded twenty others before turning the guns on themselves.

At the time, Columbine was the most deadly school shooting in US history. The nation was shocked, and many demanded Congress pass laws to close the gun-show loophole. The Senate passed a bill with provisions closing that loophole, requiring locking devices for all new handgun purchases and banning the import of high-capacity-ammunition magazines.

The NRA went to work in the House of Representatives. It enlisted two Texans—then majority whip Tom DeLay and majority leader Dick Armey—to kill the bill. In May and June the NRA spent more than $1 million on mass mailings and phone banks. NRA members wrote and phoned their members of Congress to vote against the Senate bill.

The Senate's gun package died in a House conference committee.

The NRA had honed a brilliant and effective one-two punch. It alerted members with "Armageddon Appeals." The breathless alerts described any laws or regulations as a slippery slope to confiscation. It kept the membership in a constant state of alert. In the NRA's Chicken Little world, the sky was always falling. Enough members called or wrote or accosted congressmen to weaken any intention to support strengthening our nation's gun laws.

Along with alerts, the NRA had direct access to the White

House and congressional leaders. In Washington, DC, the NRA played the lobbying game smarter and better than any other group. It hosted congressmen in a brand-new glass-enclosed office building across the Potomac River in Fairfax, Virginia—an impressive $100 million compound with more than eight hundred employees and an underground shooting range.

Flush with cash from membership contributions and gun manufacturers, the NRA's veteran leaders, LaPierre and chief lobbyist James Baker, directed campaign cash to elect friends and defeat opponents.

Even though Gabby supported the Second Amendment in Congress, she never got a dime from the NRA. And while she still has great respect for the original goals of the organization, LaPierre's Newtown speech turned her off from the NRA for good.

She frequently held social gatherings with her staff—happy hours and visits to the great memorials and monuments all over DC. The last of these informal office get-togethers before she was shot took place in the summer of 2010 at the NRA headquarters gun range in Fairfax, Virginia. Gabby and her staff had a great time at target practice before returning to DC for a few rounds of beer.

* * *

The NRA has deep pockets, and it wields its political power whenever possible. But though it can claim some great electoral shake-ups in the past, the gun-lobbying group has gradually been losing its influence over the years. Even before Newtown, the NRA spent $15 million to keep Obama from a second term in the White House, and it lost big.

As Robert Spitzer wrote in his book *The Politics of Gun*

Control, "the NRA has often sacrificed both a sense of perspective and the truth, leading to a general erosion of its credibility outside its core constituency. Unquestionably, this is a trade-off that most NRA leaders are willing to accept." Almost fifteen years after Columbine, LaPierre's post-Newtown news conference offered a high-pitched example of this trade-off.

LaPierre's speech, when viewed through this lens, also revealed a contrast that had long confused Gabby and me: the NRA's polished savvy in controlling the halls of Congress and its simultaneous appeal to extremism.

Americans have always engaged in robust debate, thanks to the First Amendment. But in the 1990s, some extremists were forming militias to train and possibly take up arms against the government. Manufacturing jobs were going abroad and unemployment was rising. Zealots portrayed federal raids on Waco and Ruby Ridge as evidence that federal agents were out of control. Strains of white supremacy and anti-Semitism laced through some militia groups. Conspiracy theorists stoked fear of the New World Order, where United Nations troops would show up in black helicopters to take over the United States and other sovereign nations and then form a single authoritarian world government.

This level of overheated fearmongering might have seemed far beyond the NRA's scope. But then we read Wayne LaPierre's take in his 2006 book *The Global War on Your Guns: Inside the U.N. Plan to Destroy the Bill of Rights,* which says, "The U.N. is the most lethal threat ever to our Second Amendment rights," adding that the organization is bent on "total gun prohibition." (And remember the insane killers and monsters and predators that LaPierre warned us against in his Newtown conference? He keeps ratcheting up the fear, because that's the brand of rhetoric that wins loyalty—and sells guns.)

Richard Feldman, a former NRA executive, describes the NRA's turn to the extreme in his book *Ricochet*. Suffering from its failure to block the Brady Bill, the NRA lost members and had to raise annual fees. Feldman writes: "the NRA cautiously began to court the militias and their far right allies."

Outlandish conspiracy theories had been knocking around the NRA for decades. Remember Neal Knox, the NRA godfather who was instrumental in blocking the organization's move to Colorado in 1977 so it could recommit to gun rights? Here's his take on the assassinations of JFK and Martin Luther King Jr. and rampages like the Stockton school shooting in 1989. "Is it possible," Knox asked in *Shotgun News*, "that some of these incidents could have been created for the purpose of disarming the people of the free world? With drugs and evil intent, it's possible. Rampant paranoia on my part? Maybe. But there have been far too many coincidences to ignore."

There has always been, and always will be, an extreme element in our society that's susceptible to these conspiracy theories. (Just try googling "Sandy Hook": one of the early suggested entries that appears on the screen is "Sandy Hook Hoax"—an elaborate theory proposing that the tragedy at Newtown was staged by gun-control activists as a pretext to seize people's guns.) Knox understood early on that his organization could benefit from aligning with this fringe.

Even if Knox's paranoia had seemed outlandish to hunters and marksmen at the time, it obviously worked, because the NRA's lean toward the extreme became part of its identity. In March 1995, the NRA ran advertisements that were hard to ignore. Full-page ads in *USA Today* and the *Washington Post* showed federal agents (or rather actors dressed as federal agents) in black SWAT gear, bursting into a home and brandishing assault weapons. The headline read: TELL THE CLINTON WHITE HOUSE TO STAY OUT OF YOUR HOUSE.

Playing off Ruby Ridge and Waco but embellishing its rhetoric, the ad warned that the Bureau of Alcohol, Tobacco and Firearms could "intensify its reign of storm trooper tactics." It described the ATF as a "rogue agency" and a "bureaucracy whose mission is to make gun ownership by definition a suspicious act, and gun owners by class suspected criminals."

The ad bore no mention of militias, but it threw gas on their flaming paranoia.

Following the full-page ads, Wayne LaPierre warned in a fundraising letter that Bill Clinton's "semiautomatic ban gives jack-booted government thugs more power to take away our Constitutional rights, break in our doors, seize our guns, destroy our property, and even injure or kill us."

He added: "Not long ago, it was unthinkable for federal agents wearing Nazi bucket helmets and black storm trooper uniforms to attack law-abiding citizens. Not today."

The ad campaign and fundraising letter landed weeks before the worst act of domestic terrorism in the nation's history. On April 19, 1995, Timothy McVeigh, an Army vet who sympathized with the militias' conspiracy theories and fears of gun control, parked a truck loaded with ammonium nitrate farm fertilizer and racing-car fuel to the north side of the Alfred P. Murrah Federal Building in downtown Oklahoma City. The truck was a massive bomb, intended to strike a blow against what McVeigh saw as the oppressive federal government.

When McVeigh walked away and tripped a fuse, the bomb

ripped away the side of the building. The blast killed 168 people and wounded more than 680. Among those who lost their lives were children in the day-care center, as well as agents with the ATF and FBI.

Trying to make some sense of the unfathomable act of violence, investigators and a grieving nation searched for McVeigh's motive. He had attended militia meetings but was not associated with any specific groups. He had been an NRA member, and Adam Winkler in his book *Gunfight* quoted one of McVeigh's friends who said he was "fanatical" about the right to bear arms.

In the months before he blew up the Murrah building, McVeigh traveled the gun-show circuit, where anti-government conspiracies were common fare. Investigators found no direct connection between McVeigh and LaPierre's "storm trooper" invective, but McVeigh shared LaPierre's demonization of the ATF.

The NRA did its best to distance itself from McVeigh and the militia movement. LaPierre offered a vague apology for the "strong and overblown" language in his fundraising letters.

George H. W. Bush was not mollified. In a letter to the NRA, the former president mentioned Al Whicher, a Secret Service agent who had served on his detail and died in McVeigh's bomb attack.

"He was no Nazi," Bush wrote. "He was a kind man, a loving parent, a man dedicated to serving his country—and serve it well he did."

Bush added that the NRA's "broadside against Federal agents deeply offends my own sense of decency and honor; and it offends my concept of service to the country."

Bush resigned his life membership in the NRA.

* * *

The NRA temporarily tamped down its extreme rhetoric in the wake of the Oklahoma City bombing, but, in looking back, we found many of its policies plenty extreme. Thanks to the NRA's prowess in Washington, some became law.

The group began to expand the scope of its lobbying beyond strictly guns and started to oppose bills designed to strengthen America's ability to fight terrorism. In response to the Oklahoma City bombing, Congress proposed a counter-terrorism bill in 1996. The NRA lobbied against provisions that would have funded studies of armor-piercing ammunition and explosives. Parts of the law would have made it easier for the government to prosecute people who provide weapons used in crimes and deport illegal aliens charged with terrorism. The NRA lobbied against these sections and successfully struck them from the weakened law that eventually passed.

Since the 9/11 terrorist attacks that killed three thousand Americans, Congress has tried to prevent individuals on the terrorist watch list from buying a weapon legally in the US. Even that proposal did not pass the NRA's political purity test, which dictates that any law or regulation to prevent anyone from buying any gun must be defeated.

If you make the terrorist watch list, you cannot board an airplane—but you can purchase an assault weapon. The FBI reported that between 2004 and 2010, 1,453 people on the terror watch list attempted to buy firearms or explosives. Of those, 90 percent were successful in their purchases. More than two hundred individuals the government suspects of having ties to terrorism legally bought guns in the US in 2010.

* * *

From space flight, I know how crucial data is. Astronauts and NASA engineers and managers rely on information that we collect, store, and analyze. The space shuttle transmits data to the ground via telemetry. We transmit information on pressure, temperature, speed, position, or voltage from thousands of components. If something broke or went wrong, we would let the data lead us to the problem and the fix. We never guessed. We didn't offer solutions that weren't based on data. Most important, we never hid or ignored the data. Precise data could mean the difference between a successful mission and failure, or even our demise.

Yet the NRA has successfully prevented the government from collecting and analyzing crucial information about guns and gun violence.

In 2003 and 2004, the NRA tacked on provisions to a larger appropriations package that greatly advance one of Wayne LaPierre's main goals: to weaken the ATF. These laws, sponsored by Kansas representative Todd Tiahrt, have blinded agencies to information that could help reduce gun violence. Sadly, they are costing lives.

One Tiahrt amendment requires the Justice Department to destroy within twenty-four hours the record of a buyer whose background check was approved. Another Tiahrt amendment bans the government from requiring gun dealers to conduct inventory checks to prevent losses or thefts. Inventory checks are a basic responsibility of all sorts of retail establishments, from bookstores to clothing boutiques— why is this practice too much to ask of gun dealers?

Every year the NRA works to keep the ATF underfunded and undermanned. In 2006 the NRA supported a bill to require that the head of the agency be confirmed by the Senate. It passed. For the next seven years, the agency had no permanent director.

Even more insane to us is that the NRA has lobbied successfully even against *studying* gun violence. Pressured by the NRA and the gun lobby, Congress has barred federal agencies from sharing information on gun violence, from its causes to its costs.

Bullets kill. More often they leave wounds. They lodge in spines or brains, they cripple, they maim for life. Headlines about deadly gun violence and mass killings grab our attention, but what about the hundreds of thousands of people who survive gunshot wounds? What are the costs to the community—the emotional tolls and the hard costs of caring for the wounded and their families?

"Medical treatment of gunshot wounds costs an estimated $2 billion annually, half of which comes from taxpayer dollars," the University of Chicago's Crime Lab wrote to Vice President Biden in January 2013 in a letter signed by 108 academics. "The total costs of gun violence to American society are on the order of $100 billion per year."

The professors and researchers called for "the removal of current barriers to firearm-related research" and direct federal investment in "unbiased scientific research" aimed at reducing gun violence.

Despite all the NRA's efforts to hamper research, some studies have produced sobering results. In 2005, the Centers for Disease Control attempted to assess the direct medical costs of treating fatal gun injuries, combined with the economic damage of lost lives. It estimated the price tag at $37 billion. The CDC reported that nonfatal injuries cost an additional $3.7 billion.

The Pacific Institute for Research and Evaluation, a non-profit independent research group, pegged the cost of firearm injuries in the United States at $174 billion in 2010. The institute assessed the costs of medical and mental health care, emergency services, criminal justice costs, wage losses, and insurance, as well as pain and suffering. The Pacific Institute conducted one of the most far-reaching studies yet, but we need far more data, research, and education on the costs of gun violence.

If the NRA has its way, that will never happen.

*　*　*

You might think the first word in the organization's name—*National*—indicates the scope of the NRA's activities. Brazil, surely, is too far afield for the NRA to insert itself. You would be wrong.

In 2006, Brazilians voted on a referendum that would have established a nationwide gun ban. Brazil's large cities have rough neighborhoods beset by gun violence. The nation's gun-death rate ranks among the highest in the world.

Early national polls showed more than 70 percent of Brazilians supported the gun ban. Nevertheless, NRA strategists showed up in Brazil as early as 2003 to work against the gun ban, David Morton wrote for *Foreign Policy* magazine in 2006. These US advisors helped gun-rights activists refocus the debate. Taking a page from their US game plan, they stoked fears that the Brazilian government would begin with guns and proceed to encroach on other rights.

The gun-ban referendum failed.

"We view Brazil as the opening salvo for the global gun-control movement," NRA spokesman Andrew Arulanandam said after the vote. "If gun proponents succeed in Brazil, America will be next."

The NRA has also fought gun laws in Australia, Britain, Canada, and New Zealand.

Worldwide, the illegal sale of small arms is a big problem. They are responsible for at least half a million deaths a year. The United Nations has been trying to control the illicit small-arms trade for decades, and for decades the NRA has opposed it, going back to 2001, when President George W. Bush reversed Bill Clinton's support for restricting international arms trafficking.

"To the bewilderment of representatives from other countries," Spitzer writes, "the Bush administration argued that such a UN effort would not only impinge on American gun habits but also on the US Constitution's Second Amendment."

The UN recently approved an international arms treaty, but senators backed by the NRA have vowed to oppose it. The United States could stand in the way of a treaty that could save lives worldwide.

* * *

By taking a deep look at the full scope of the NRA's activities, Gabby and I understood how and why the NRA has been so successful at controlling gun laws and regulations.

The group's greatest strength lies in its ability to mobilize members to influence every debate on guns. The NRA today claims five million members, and it is in touch with them constantly, trumpeting semifactual reports and issuing alarmist alerts. It calls on members to contact politicians, and many respond with letters, calls, and e-mails. In 2010, the NRA spent $57 million communicating with members. That represents nearly a quarter of its budget.

The NRA uses funds to get access on Capitol Hill, reward allies, and punish opponents. In the last three federal elections, it has contributed $3.3 million directly to candidates and spent $44 million on independent expenditures, meaning it could run its own ads and send direct mail in support of its favored candidates. Since 1998, the group has spent $31.6 million lobbying in Washington, according to OpenSecrets.org and the Federal Election Commission. The NRA deploys between sixteen and thirty-five lobbyists, depending on the year and its legislative agenda.

The NRA's agenda prevailed even in the first term of Barack Obama's presidency. Though the organization had repeatedly (and profitably) warned its followers that the president would soon be "coming for our guns," Obama had actually loosened several gun restrictions in the years before Newtown. Though Amtrak had barred guns on trains after the September 11, 2001, terrorist attacks, in September 2009 Congress passed a bill that allowed passengers on Amtrak trains to put weapons in checked bags. Gabby—who fought for the rights of responsible gun owners—also supported this bill, as well as one passed the same year that reversed a twenty-five-year ban on guns in national parks. (The first bill was part of a larger appropriations package that she approved.)

The NRA even pushed to get a provision added to President Obama's health care legislation that stopped health care insurers from charging people who owned guns more for coverage.

As this wide-ranging legislation suggests, the NRA has had its way in Washington for decades. We can't help but admire its loyal membership and mastery of the political process.

But the group's history of successes has obscured the fact that even many of its five million members increasingly believe the group has gone too far, especially when it comes to its opposition to expanded background checks for gun purchases. A study in January 2013 by Johns Hopkins University found that 74 percent of people who identified themselves as NRA members support universal background checks for gun sales. Surveys by the Pew Research Center and Gallup had similar results.

Wayne LaPierre's proposal for arming school security guards in response to the Newtown rampage might have succeeded in appealing to the fringe, but the rest of America decided that this time the NRA had gone too far. Like many law-abiding gun owners across the country, Gabby and I were appalled by LaPierre's violent, irresponsible language. Once again, the NRA had gone too far with its scare tactics—and this time, we were determined to bring some sanity back to the debate.

CHAPTER EIGHT

NRA, INC.

Political meddling is one thing, but there's another side to the NRA that Gabby and I began to find even more troubling.

The National Rifle Association, you'll recall, was founded as a gun safety group in the aftermath of the Civil War, an organization aimed at schooling urban Northern soldiers in the basics of marksmanship. Today, the NRA maintains affiliations with youth organizations like the Boy Scouts and 4-H, and since 1988, its Eddie Eagle GunSafe program has taught young Americans how to protect themselves if they stumble upon a gun. We are the first to admit that, through these and other programs, the NRA does a great job of promoting gun safety.

But the NRA is also, historically, an advocacy group for gun owners. From the NRA's point of view, owning a gun is a basic civil right, and therefore the NRA is a civil rights group—as the homepage of the organization's website puts it, "America's longest-standing civil-rights organization."

Though the NRA has fairly high approval ratings, and most Americans see the group in a positive light, Gabby and I always sensed that the NRA was more than a benign advocacy group for gun owners.

I was especially curious about the relationship between the NRA and gun manufacturers, which I assumed was close. To understand the issues, policy, and laws around gun rights and gun violence, we first had to investigate the ties between the NRA and the firearms industry.

Did the firearms industry control the NRA? Was that why LaPierre's organization was so dead set against even the most basic regulations on guns?

The answers came as a great surprise to me and Gabby.

* * *

In 1999, cities across the country started suing the firearms industry for damages caused by gun violence.

"By taking this action," said Mayor Joseph Ganim of Bridgeport, Connecticut, "we are saying to the handgun industry, 'From now on, you are responsible for the costs associated with your handgun products.'"

Mayors filed lawsuits based on the legal theory that gun makers were responsible for violence that was costing cities millions of dollars in law enforcement and medical care. The gun makers, they argued, were liable for negligence and creating a public nuisance by making deadly weapons coveted by criminals. Municipalities also targeted gun dealers for selling weapons they allegedly knew were destined for street violence.

The theories seemed to be a stretch: why would a firearms manufacturer like Glock or a gun shop be responsible for damages caused by a handgun used in a street crime? But there was an interesting precedent, as in recent years states had successfully sued tobacco companies for the health care costs of treating cigarette smokers. Major tobacco companies had just agreed to settle lawsuits by paying upward of $200 billion to the states. Why not try to apply similar legal theories to gun makers and make them compensate cities and states for millions associated with footing the bills for gun violence?

Philadelphia Mayor Ed Rendell told the *Philadelphia Inquirer* in the summer of 1999 that his lawyers were preparing a lawsuit against the whole "firearms industry" to recoup costs to the city for "gun crime." Add up the costs of public-safety budgets, ambulance runs, and hospital services, and you have hundreds of millions of dollars just for Philadelphia, he said.

New Orleans Mayor Marc Morial announced in the fall of 1998 that he was also preparing a lawsuit against the industry. The National Center to Prevent Handgun Violence joined the legal fray and asked the same consortium of lawyers who had successfully sued Big Tobacco to lead the litigation. Around the same time, Chicago sued gun dealers in the suburbs for $433 million for selling guns to undercover officers dressed as gang members. The investigators had videotaped dealers selling guns to ineligible buyers.

The cities were encouraged by a New York case in which a Brooklyn jury awarded monetary damages to families of gun-violence victims. The families claimed that the manufacturers of weapons used in the shootings had been negligent in their marketing and distribution methods. The jury agreed with the claim that the companies somehow knew the guns would be used in street crimes. This was a stretch, and an appeals court overturned the verdict.

That didn't stop nearly thirty cities from bringing suit against gun makers.

"Gun makers must shoulder the costs that taxpayers have carried alone until now," said Mayor Alex Penelas of Miami-

151

Dade County. "But more importantly, they must make dramatic changes to protect the unintended victims of their deadly products."

The National Rifle Association saw these lawsuits as a potentially mortal threat to its principal partner and patron, the firearms industry.

At Wayne LaPierre's insistence, the NRA had elected actor Charlton Heston as its president in 1998. Heston's role was largely ceremonial, but he would prove to be a powerful voice for LaPierre. In a speech to the industry's biggest trade show the next year, the actor who had played Moses and Ben-Hur made the NRA's intentions toward the embattled firearms industry clear.

"For a century, we have thrived independently," Heston said. "But now your fight has become our fight."

*   *   *

But Heston's claim of independence turned out to be a joke—though one with a very different punch line than the one Gabby and I saw coming. The NRA and the firearms industry had been intimately connected for over a century. For decades, owners of firearms firms have sat on the NRA's board of directors, proving that the revolving door between the industry and the NRA operates at the very highest levels.

The shock, to Gabby and me, was the direction the power flowed. We had assumed that the big gun manufacturers controlled the NRA. We were wrong.

Of course, even in the early days of ARS, we had started to pick up some hints about who was really in charge. We spoke to many gun-shop owners, both near our home in Tucson and over the summer of 2013, when we took a trip across Nevada, Alaska, North Dakota, and New Hampshire. All over the country, we interviewed gun-shop owners about our commonsense proposals to curb gun violence. Almost all of them agreed that with a few reasonable measures, we could protect the Second Amendment while keeping Americans safer from gun violence.

The catch was that almost no one would speak to us on the record. The reason for their requests of anonymity? These businessmen were afraid of incurring the wrath of the NRA.

And to be honest, they were right to be afraid. The NRA has initiated a boycott of at least one gun manufacturer that fell out of line with its hard line on gun ownership for all. It doesn't matter how passionately these people—who make their living manufacturing and selling guns, after all—believe in the Second Amendment. Speaking out against the NRA could quickly send a gun-shop owner or even a massive fire-arm manufacturer into bankruptcy proceedings. If you want to stay in business, you toe the NRA line, period.

Just look at what happened to the iconic gun maker Smith & Wesson in 2000, when the company tried to respond to public calls for safer guns in the wake of those liability lawsuits from twenty-nine different cities. Smith & Wesson CEO Ed Shultz entered talks with the federal government and agreed to some basic safety measures on its handguns: a lock, no magazines with more than ten rounds, and a more thorough system of background checks.

The result? Fury from the NRA. In a press release titled "The Smith & Wesson Sellout," the group condemned Smith & Wesson for being "the first gun maker to run up the white flag of surrender" to the Clinton administration. Worse than that, the NRA initiated a boycott, and Smith & Wesson's sales plummeted by 40 percent. The company closed two factories and barely survived.

Smith & Wesson learned its lesson and loudly renounced the safety agreement by introducing a new high-powered gun. The NRA eventually welcomed the prodigal son back, and by 2010, Smith & Wesson had returned from the dead and was making record profits with sales of high-powered rifles. One of these guns, fitted with an "ultra-capacity magazine" containing one hundred rounds, was used in the Aurora, Colorado, shooting in July of 2012.

Moral of the story: the NRA had flexed its muscles, and it had won.

* * *

The NRA is kept afloat by lots and lots of money, much of it coming from corporate contributions from the firearms industry. That's because, even if it once was a "civil rights organization," the NRA is now essentially a trade organization, and—as Smith & Wesson learned the hard way—its member parties have a lot riding on keeping the big guns like LaPierre happy.

Corporate contributions are a big reason the NRA has so much money to spend influencing the outcome of elections: corporations that manufacture guns, ammunition, or weapons parts and accessories have contributed as much as $53 million to the NRA since 2005 through its Ring of Freedom sponsorship program. At its annual meeting in May 2013, the NRA celebrated the entry of Smith & Wesson—the company that, just over a decade earlier, it had come very close to destroying—into the program's Golden Ring of Freedom for donations exceeding $1 million.

Other million-dollar industry donors honored at the event were Brownells and Freedom Group, manufacturer of the Bushmaster assault rifle used in the Newtown tragedy.

Beretta and Ruger have topped $1 million to the sponsorship program.

In addition to benefitting from the financial success of firearms companies, the NRA also directly benefits from individual gun sales. Corporate "partners" can participate in the NRA Round-Up program, where gun buyers can round their purchase up to the next dollar, and the difference goes to the NRA. MidwayUSA, a distributor of high-capacity magazines and other firearm accessories, reports on its website that it has donated about $9.4 million to the NRA by rounding up. Through the Add a Buck program, gun buyers can throw in an extra dollar to a sale, which goes directly to the NRA.

Crimson Trace, a major manufacturer of laser sights, describes itself as "an NRA Company" on its website. Supporting the NRA is an "absolute," the company says, and notes that 100 percent of its employees are NRA members. Crimson Trace offers laser sights featuring the NRA logo, and it sends 10 percent of the purchase price of these special sights back to the NRA.

Sturm, Ruger & Co., the country's fourth-largest firearms maker, came up with the most direct connection between a gun sale and NRA coffers by way of its "One Million Gun Challenge." Ruger CEO Mike Fifer told customers in 2011 that if his company broke a firearms-industry record and sold a million guns in the next year, it would present the NRA with a check for $1 million, a dollar a gun.

"With the help of America's gun buyers," Fifer said, "we hope to make history and to share that accomplishment with the NRA." Ruger exceeded its goal and presented the NRA with a check for $1.254 million.

* * *

These contributions might look hefty on paper, but they're a small price to pay for the protections offered by the NRA. Remember all the lawsuits by the mayors back in 1999? Well, once the NRA "took up the fight" of the embattled gun makers, they no longer had to worry.

The NRA did as promised, and LaPierre and chief NRA lobbyist Chris Cox mounted a legislative defense of the firearms industry. It deployed all of its lobbying and legislative resources in a battle that raged through the back corridors of Capitol Hill and statehouses across the nation for six years.

On October 30, 1998, New Orleans became the first city to sue gun makers. Charging that gun manufacturers had avoided new technologies, such as child-safety locks, that could have made their products safer, the city filed suit against fifteen handgun manufacturers, including Glock, Smith & Wesson, and Beretta.

"This suit is about holding that very successful industry accountable," Mayor Marc Morial said at a city hall press conference.

The NRA and industry executives argued that lawsuits like the New Orleans case would drive many smaller companies into bankruptcy. That became more possible when thirty different state and local governments followed the lead of New Orleans and filed suit or threatened legal action. In June 2000 both New York City and New York State filed suit against the gun makers. Rudy Giuliani, then mayor of New York, became the first Republican to sue the industry.

For the NRA, settling the suits was a nonstarter—just look at what happened when Smith & Wesson promised to change their practices.

As soon as New Orleans took legal action against the firearms industry, the NRA moved to neutralize the threat. It marshaled its lobbyists in state capitals and in Congress. Passing laws that would shield the industry from lawsuits by cities and states became the NRA's top legislative priority. These laws would preempt cities from suing gun firms or dealers. In short, suing gun makers and dealers would be illegal.

Over the next six years, the NRA worked tirelessly in statehouses all over the country, and by 2005 thirty-three states had passed legislation barring localities from suing gun makers or dealers. But the group devoted its most intense lobbying, directed by Wayne LaPierre, to Capitol Hill.

Idaho Senator Larry Craig, a longtime NRA board member, led the charge on the inside. "The cost of these lawsuits threatens to drive a critical industry out of business," Craig said, "jeopardizing Americans' constitutionally protected access to firearms for self-defense and other lawful uses."

The House passed a bill to provide federal liability protection for gun makers in 2003. A year later the Senate passed its version, but gun-control proponents added amendments to extend the assault-weapons ban, to require background checks for all purchases at gun shows, and to require safety locks on new handguns. The NRA balked at the poison pills. It withdrew its support, instructed its Senate allies to vote against the amended legislation, and the bill died, 90 to 8.

"They had the power to turn around at least sixty votes in the Senate," California Senator Dianne Feinstein told the *New York Times*. "That's amazing to me."

"I've been around here eighteen years," Senator John McCain said, "and I've never seen anything quite this bizarre."

But a year later, with more Republicans supportive of gun rights in Congress, a bill to shield gun makers passed both the House and Senate. President Bush quickly signed the Protection of Lawful Commerce in Arms Act of 2005. It blocked civil lawsuits against gun makers, dealers, distributors, and importers of ammunition and firearms. They could no longer be held liable for negligence if the products they manufactured or sold were used in crimes. If, however, a manufacturer made defective guns or a dealer *knowingly* sold a weapon to someone not legally able to own a gun, they could still be sued.

The passage of the law had an immediate effect. It halted more than a dozen ongoing cases against the gun industry. And it frustrated any future attempts to match the legal actions states had taken against the tobacco companies. Judges had already dismissed many of the cases brought by cities, including Chicago's lawsuit against suburban gun dealers.

Wayne LaPierre and the NRA took credit for the new law. "History will show," LaPierre said, "that this law helped save the American firearms industry from collapse under the burden of these ruinous and politically motivated lawsuits." Victims of gun violence were no longer able to sue the makers of the guns used against them, and the arms industry could celebrate.

The donations came flooding in.

* * *

But the relationship between the NRA and its biggest benefactor, the firearms industry, isn't always so seamless. More and more, the NRA's positions on a range of issues falls far to the right of the industry it's so devoted to protecting.

That's because, whatever the NRA might claim, gun manufacturers are on the whole a moderate bunch. They see no conflict between the Second Amendment and law and order. After all, firearms makers get some of their biggest contracts from law-enforcement and government agencies.

They don't profit when gun traffickers sell their products on the black market, or when mentally ill people obtain guns and put them to terrible use. Truth be told, gun manufacturers make the most money when people shop at gun stores, where background checks are conducted. That's because people who shop in gun stores are more likely to load up on accessories, and firearm accessories have much higher profit margins than the guns themselves. So from a profit standpoint, manufacturers do best when weapons are purchased through an FFL, or federally licensed firearm dealer.

So one might assume that gun makers would come out in support of universal background checks, right?

Well, according to an article by Paul Barrett in *Businessweek* titled "Why Gun Makers Fear the NRA," in the weeks after Newtown major firearms makers contacted the NRA—not to "issue directives." Instead, Barrett wrote, "they sought guidance on how to handle the public-relations crisis, according to people familiar with the situation who agreed to interviews on the condition they remain anonymous."

There it is again: all sources must remain anonymous. As we would later experience firsthand on our cross-country trip, people whose livelihood depends on making and selling guns are not about to make these opinions known for fear of angering their chief protector, the NRA. Though gun makers tend to have more moderate views because of their contracts with law enforcement, they cannot show their stripes for fear of angering the NRA.

And let's not forget that gun manufacturers directly benefit from the brand of hyped-up paranoia that LaPierre uses so effectively, most memorably at his post-Newtown press conference. This tactic has served LaPierre and his patron well for years. After LaPierre's unhinged-seeming performance that December, the guns started flying off the shelves, and profits soared.

By this point, we should all be familiar with the NRA's time-tested methods. Step one: incite fear. Step two: urge people to buy guns. Step three: fill the NRA's coffers with the arms industry's profits. As we've seen over and over, the NRA uses any effort to regulate guns, real or imagined, to stir fears of imminent gun confiscation. And the more scared people are, the more guns they buy.

"We live in the most dangerous of times," LaPierre advised the faithful at the NRA's 2012 convention in St. Louis, eight months before Newtown. He painted a bleak picture of an America beset by terrorists, vulnerable to natural disasters, and verging on the brink of an "unprecedented breakdown of social order."

Well, Gabby and I have a different view. We think Americans are too smart to be manipulated into a state of permanent fear. We see this country as a place where people gather together to solve problems as a community. We shoulder sandbags to avert floods and help our loved ones through hard times. We join forces with neighbors and total strangers to come to the aid of those in need after catastrophes. Cooperation and collaboration are part of the fabric of our nation.

The NRA makes a good deal of money promoting a more pessimistic vision. "People are anticipating dangerous times and are responding in the only sensible, logical way possible," LaPierre proclaimed. "They're buying guns!"

People have been buying guns from venerable American arms makers since George Washington helped establish the Springfield Armory in Massachusetts in 1777. Entrepreneurs and gun manufacturers like Samuel Colt, Eli Whitney, Oliver Winchester, and John Browning became legends.

They helped build a great industry that supplied American soldiers with the best weapons in the world. They continue to manufacture the finest rifles and shotguns for hunting, target shooting, and recreation, as well as handguns for self-protection.

And thanks in large part to the NRA, the making and selling of firearms and accessories in the US is now an $11.7 billion industry. This is not a bad thing. The strength of the firearms industry is great for our economy: the National Shooting Sports Foundation says the arms industry contributes $33 billion to the US economy and supports about 220,000 jobs. Based on estimates by federal officials and FBI background checks, firearms sales are rising.

But there are threats to the continued health of the industry. For one, firearms don't break down; they last. A good gun is expertly made from the strongest materials by top craftsmen. And while it's true that sales and profits from firearms are rising, the rate of gun ownership in America has been steadily dropping, according to the General Social Survey.

Basic demographics are working against the industry. Fewer than 38 percent of Americans born after 1980 report having a gun in their home. With more Americans living in suburbs and cities, there are fewer hunters. As recently as 2008, rifles and shotguns for hunting represented nearly half of firearm sales. That number has dropped to 25 percent and is projected to keep falling.

America is becoming safer. Crime rates are down across the nation, including the rate of gun-related murder and manslaughter, according to the National Institute of Justice.

So what explains the rising weapon sales and profits? It might have come, in part, from what gun executives call the "Obama surge" created by the National Rifle Association.

Since Obama's election in 2008, and even more so since his reelection in 2012, the NRA has been pushing a narrative of the president as a "gun grabber" who would usher in a new era of gun restrictions.

But Obama did nothing to restrict gun ownership in his first term and actually expanded gun rights, signing laws to allow guns in national parks and on Amtrak trains.

But reality has never had a big impact on LaPierre's conspiracy theories. In the run-up to the 2012 election, LaPierre wrote to NRA members that Obama "has spent his entire political career—over 16 years—proposing, promoting, or secretly supporting the most radical and anti-firearm-freedom policies you can imagine."

Gun owners continued to respond exactly as LaPierre hoped they would: by buying more weapons. During Obama's first term, industry-wide sales rose 30 percent to $4.3 billion, according to *Businessweek*. Gun websites jokingly called the president the "Gun Salesman of the Year." And it's true that the figures since he took office are startling, to judge by a 2012 Associated Press analysis of how the two biggest gun makers in the US had fared since Obama had taken office: Sturm, Ruger & Company's profits had risen 86 percent, and Smith & Wesson's had jumped 44 percent.

* * *

We have immense regard for America's firearms industry, its workers, and their contributions to our communities. We believe the industry can thrive even with reasonable changes to laws, especially universal background checks.

As it stands now, the NRA has fostered the fear-based market that encourages people to clear shelves, even after massacres like Aurora or the Tucson shooting that nearly

162

killed Gabby. Even after Newtown. For LaPierre, the only possible answer to the problem of gun violence is more guns. Because the more guns people buy, the more money and power trickles down to LaPierre and his organization. Rather than protecting the Second Amendment, the NRA appears to be protecting profits first.

But the free market might soon become a problem for these firms. Many investors are seeking to withdraw their funds from firearms companies that object to reasonable gun laws.

The California teachers' pension fund had invested millions in the private equity firm Cerberus Capital Management. Cerberus had a significant stake in Freedom Group, the parent company of Bushmaster, the maker of the AR-15 used by Adam Lanza. After the slaughter of children and educators in Newtown, the teachers pressured Cerberus to divest its investments in the gun business.

After the Sandy Hook shootings, Tiger Global Management, a major hedge fund, quietly sold its stake in Ruger, saying it would no longer invest in firearms firms. Around the same time, the California Public Employees' Retirement System, the largest US pension fund, sold its stakes in Smith & Wesson and Ruger. Public pension funds from many major cities—among them New York, Los Angeles, Philadelphia, and Chicago—committed to pulling back their investments from firearms makers who profit from assault weapons and high-capacity ammunition magazines.

Minneapolis Mayor R.T. Rybak proposed in January after the Newtown shootings that cities across the country use their buying power as leverage to push for laws designed to reduce gun violence. "We buy a lot of guns and ammunition," Rybak told a city council committee. "We should really question whether the companies that we are buying from are going to Washington and are working with us or fighting against us."

Rybak said Minneapolis has spent nearly $800,000 on guns and ammunition in the previous eight years. He and mayors from sixty cities are examining their contracts with companies that supply their law-enforcement officers with guns and ammunition, Rybak said.

"If we find out they're not partners," he said, "and if we find out they're working against us, then we all ought to have a conversation as taxpayers about whether our dollars should be used for people who are not working to reduce gun violence."

For decades, the NRA and the arms industry have mutually benefited from their financial and political alliance. But the political and financial terrain is changing fast.

If firearms manufacturers continue to oppose background checks and refuse to consider any new laws to curb gun violence, they might find out their politics are bad for business.

CHAPTER NINE

A BROKEN SYSTEM

G iven the power of the NRA, we knew we had to work harder to keep guns out of the hands of the wrong people—but how? The more we learned, the more complicated the answer became. There were no quick fixes. The damage done by firearms in America goes far beyond the headline-grabbing mass shootings like Tucson, Aurora, and Newtown, but too many of us have become numb to the daily carnage.

Every day, gun violence in America claims 270 victims on average, according to the Centers for Disease Control: of those, eighty-six die, thirty-one of them murder victims. (The rest are mostly suicide and some accidents, equally tragic.) An analysis by the Violence Policy Center showed that in 2010, gun deaths outpaced motor-vehicle deaths in twelve states and the District of Columbia as the leading cause of death. Arizona recorded 795 motor-vehicle deaths while guns killed 931. In Michigan, 1,076 died by gunfire and 1,063 perished in motor-vehicle accidents. Virginia: 875 by guns, 728 in vehicles. In January 2013, the online magazine *Slate* began a daily tracking of US gun deaths in the wake of Newtown. By Memorial Day of 2013, it counted 4,987 people who had died as a result of gunfire in just five months. That's more U.S. casualties than in the entire Iraq War.

We can use these shockingly high numbers to make our point, but it was the human tragedies behind the gun violence that haunted Gabby and me. Just a month and a half after Newtown, my wife and I mourned the senseless death of fifteen-year-old Hadiya Pendleton, who was shot in her neighborhood of Chicago, where death by gunfire had reached epidemic levels. Hadiya was a member of her high school's majorette team that had traveled to Washington, DC, earlier that month to perform in Barack Obama's second inaugural celebration. Days later she was gunned down in Chicago, an innocent bystander to gang violence. By Fourth of July weekend of last year—when seventy-four people were shot and twelve killed—Chicago had surpassed two hundred homicides for the year, most of them gun related.

"This is not the America we strive for," Gabby and I tweeted after Hadiya's death.

It seemed that we weren't the only Americans who had finally vowed to work toward reducing gun violence. Newtown had woken up the whole country. For the first time in decades, some of our political leaders, gun-company financiers, the media, and the general public were professing an openness to improving our gun laws.

In the early months of 2013, Gabby and I watched as Congress and the White House tried to tackle the political complexities of gun-violence prevention. In those raw weeks after Newtown, President Obama had asked Vice President Joe Biden to lead a commission to study gun violence, which led to the White House proposing and issuing executive orders on gun policy and enforcement.

Prominent members of the Senate were also taking on various aspects of the issue: Senator Dianne Feinstein was working on a bill to reinstate an assault-weapons ban while Senator Patrick Leahy was focused on strengthening laws against gun trafficking. Senator Kirsten Gillibrand, a good friend of Gabby's, introduced her own gun-trafficking legislation; others circulated a bill to limit high-capacity magazines.

Gabby and I paid attention to all of these developments as we began to put together our organization. From the very beginning, we were pragmatic in our goals. Could we bring gun violence to a complete halt? Of course not. But by focusing on a few specific measures that gun owners, law-enforcement officers, and Americans from across the political spectrum approved of, we could join with like-minded citizens to put the nation on a better course.

But what was the best approach to take? Gabby and I wanted to focus on issues that felt true to our core beliefs. Both of us are moderates. In Congress, Gabby, a former Republican, was conservative on some issues, more liberal on others.

As a military officer, I had been fairly apolitical for most of my adult life. I believed in serving my commander in chief regardless of party affiliation. And I could relate to people from all over the country: although I grew up in New Jersey, I consider myself rooted in the Southwest, having lived in Texas and now Arizona for nearly two decades.

Gabby and I are also gun owners, and our belief in the Second Amendment has always been central to our lives. We wanted to stake out territory in the sensible middle ground— a lonely territory in the gun debate. Finding points of agreement with reasonable people on all sides of the issue was the core of our mission in those early days, and it remains so today.

America needs balance as it builds its laws for the future, and we wanted to create a formidable organization that would grow and thrive, just as the gun lobby had done over the last six decades.

From the very beginning, we were determined to play an active role in political and policy debates. To do that, we knew we needed to raise enough money so that our voices would be heard on Capitol Hill and in statehouses. We also wanted to help candidates in political campaigns who were committed to improving our gun laws, and oppose those who were working against sensible policies.

One of our first moves was to create a political organization called a Super PAC. With it we could advocate for or against a political candidate, but we could not work directly with that candidate. We also formed an organization known as a 501(c)(4) that could weigh in on issues and educate our leaders on them—essentially an advocacy organization that would do the tough policy work in DC and in the state capitals.

With our founding staff and donors, we established a lean organization that we hope will remain part of the national conversation for decades to come. And we built it around a few critical priorities Gabby and I had always embraced— and that the overwhelming majority of Americans supported as well.

*   *   *

Gabby and I had long believed that the main problem was not the hardware itself, like the type of gun, but the type of person in possession of the gun. We don't fundamentally disagree with the NRA's constantly repeated line, "Guns don't kill people. People kill people." But our country is in a state of crisis, especially compared to other developed nations, precisely because we have few measures in place to keep guns out of the hands of people who *do* kill.

Take the stalker and dating violence gaps, which early on became a focus of our organization. As it currently stands, people with misdemeanor domestic violence convictions are prohibited from owning a firearm, while those with misdemeanor stalking convictions (and many charges are dropped down to this misdemeanor category), or those who have misdemeanor convictions for domestic violence against dating partners, are not. Why this inconsistency? After all, don't most of us agree that dangerous criminals shouldn't have access to firearms? So why aren't we doing more—much, much more—to keep guns out of the hands of convicted stalkers and known domestic abusers?

In 2005, 40 percent of female homicide victims in this country were killed by a current or former partner, with guns used in more than half of those murders. According to the Law Center to Prevent Gun Violence, "abused women were five times as likely to be killed by their abuser if the abuser owns a firearm." And domestic-violence conflicts when a gun is involved were *twenty-three times* more likely to result in death than assaults with other weapons.

In many of these cases, the perpetrators had a previous record of stalking or harassing the women who were to become their victims. Even though federal law bans domestic abusers subject to certain restraining orders from possessing firearms along with those who have misdemeanor domestic-violence convictions, people can easily skirt these laws—with fatal consequences.

The story of Zina Haughton is both tragic and far too common. In October 2012, Haughton obtained a restraining order against her husband, Radcliffe, telling a Wisconsin court that his threats "terrorize my every waking moment." The court granted the restraining order, which made her husband ineligible to purchase a gun under federal law.

But Radcliffe Haughton was able to skirt that law without much difficulty. He searched for a gun on the Internet and found a private seller on the website Armslist—which its founder described as "a gun show that never ends"—willing to do business. Under current law, federally licensed dealers must pass prospective purchasers through the system that would have turned Haughton down. But the private dealer was not legally required to check on Haughton's background.

The gun seller met Haughton in a McDonald's parking lot and sold him a handgun for $500. He took the weapon to the Azana Salon & Spa in suburban Milwaukee where Zina worked and proceeded to open fire at the pedicure station, killing his wife and two of her coworkers. He wounded four others before he shot himself.

We need to do more to protect women like Zina Haughton from the abusers stalking and threatening them. We are working to change the law to expand protections for potential victims. At the moment, the federal gun prohibition against domestic abusers only applies if the couple has been married, lived together, or had a child together. We should expand those categories to include dating partners as well. We are also working to prohibit people convicted of a stalking misdemeanor from obtaining guns.

These measures will do nothing to curtail the rights of responsible citizens, but they will keep guns out of the hands of dangerous people, and Gabby and I believe that's a goal worth fighting for.

* * *

We also need *far* better measures to keep people with known mental illnesses from obtaining guns—an example of a point where we can reach agreement with people on every side of the gun-control debate, including the NRA.

Like Jared Loughner, Seung-Hui Cho was known among his friends and schoolmates as a troubled young man. He frightened teachers and classmates at Virginia Tech with his violent and macabre writings. He talked about suicide.

But Cho differed from Loughner in one crucial way: the authorities *knew* he was sick and potentially dangerous. When Cho, a senior at Virginia Tech, e-mailed a room-mate and said he might as well kill himself, the roommate called the police. They brought Cho to the New River Valley Community Services Board, the mental health agency that serves Blacksburg, Virginia, where the Virginia Tech campus is located. A counselor assessed Cho and found him "mentally ill and in need of hospitalization." The next day, on December 14, 2005, a judge declared Cho mentally ill and in imminent danger to himself. He ordered him into involuntary outpatient treatment.

But neither the counselor's assessment nor the judge's determination made its way into the Justice Department's NICS system. NICS stands for National Instant Criminal Background Check System, and it's used to determine whether a prospective buyer has any criminal record or history of mental illness (or any other disqualifying condition) that should prevent him from owning a firearm.

If the state had shared its disturbing reports with NICS, Cho would have been prevented from buying guns from a gun dealer. Moreover, Cho never received treatment for his mental illness, according to Virginia health and judicial authorities. No one enforced the judge's 2005 order that

Cho get treatment, and no one in the state's mental health system followed through.

And so, with his troubled mental health history unreported to the NICS database, in 2007 Cho purchased two semiautomatic pistols from a licensed dealer. He bought bullets online through eBay. On April 26 of that year he used them to kill thirty-two people and wound seventeen others on the Virginia Tech campus before shooting himself in the head. It remains the most deadly shooting incident by a single gunman in US history.

If Virginia had shared its reports of Cho's mental illness, he would have been barred from buying guns, at least from a federally licensed dealer. As it was, he encountered no obstacles on the road to mass murder. If he had received treatment, like the judge had ordered, perhaps he could have been stopped before it was too late.

To prevent another tragedy like the one at Virginia Tech, we want to see states share the appropriate mental health records with NICS so the database can be more complete and effective.

Even Wayne LaPierre claims to support this measure: "We have a mental health system in this country that has completely and totally collapsed," he told NBC after the Newtown rampage. "We have no national database of these lunatics. Twenty-three states are still putting only a small number of records into the system, and a lot of states are putting none."

After the Virginia Tech massacre, Congress passed the NICS Improvement Amendments Act, which incentivized states to do a better job of sharing mental health records with the federal system. Virginia increased the flow of records and had submitted more than 180,000 by the fall of 2012, according to *USA Today*. Eighteen states passed laws after the Virginia Tech shooting to share records. Indiana passed a law in 2009 that requires state courts to submit records of anyone found mentally ill during judicial proceedings to NICS. Texas passed a similar law that went deeper by combing twenty years of past records to include anyone who had been committed to a mental institution or been determined to be dangerous. Texas submitted more than 209,150 records to NICS by the end of 2012. By April 2013, New Jersey had added the names of 420,000 current and former residents who have been involuntarily committed to psychiatric facilities to NICS.

The Government Accountability Office reported that mental health records in the NICS system increased eightfold from 2004 to 2011. As of January 2014, the NICS system had three million records, one million of which were submitted in 2013. That represents real progress—but it's not enough. There are still far too many loopholes.

Just look at the current situation in our home state of Arizona. While Arizona has a state law that mandates reporting people declared a danger to themselves or others and prohibits those people from owning a gun, no law requires that information be reported to the federal government. And because the process of reporting is expensive and complicated—and differs state by state—many state authorities still don't submit mental health records to NICS. This results in many dangerous loopholes; for example, a person with known mental health problems in one state can just cross the border into the next state to buy a gun.

In Arizona, Jared Loughner didn't even have to go to that much trouble. Though there was no question that he suffered from mental illness—Pima Community College had

173

expelled him because of his mental instability—that crucial piece of information never became part of the database for firearm background checks, so Loughner passed.

Loughner had never been legally adjudicated as mentally ill, meaning no court had found him dangerously mentally ill or involuntarily committed him to a mental health facility. And even if state officials *had* declared him mentally ill, Loughner might still have passed a federal background check. That's because, at the time of Gabby's shooting, Arizona had more than 121,000 records of people with mental illness that had not been submitted to the federal NICS system.

What if Pima Community College had had systems in place to refer Loughner for adjudication, and he'd actually been assessed by a court or a mental health professional? Then yes, we contend that Jared Loughner would have failed the background check and been unable to buy a gun from a dealer with a federal firearms license. But unfortunately, as in so many other states, he could have skirted the background check altogether by purchasing his weapon at a gun show or over the Internet.

* * *

Gun trafficking was another major problem that Gabby and I wanted to prioritize.

Let's say you want to make some extra cash selling guns. You have no criminal record and pass a background check at a licensed firearms dealer. You buy ten inexpensive handguns for about $200 each. You load them into your trunk, drive to a street corner late at night, and sell the pistols for $400 each to a customer base that may consist of criminals, but you don't have direct knowledge of their activities one way or the other.

With your markup, you make $2,000. As you drive off, you toss an empty paper cup from your window. "What crime was committed here?" a report by Third Way, a moderate think tank, asks. Answer: "Littering."

That's right: there are no federal laws that make those gun transactions illegal. If we applied the same lax standards to drug dealing, a person caught holding dozens of small baggies of cocaine on a street corner late at night would only be charged with possession, not the far more serious charge of intent to distribute.

But by contrast, many laws on the books actually *hamper* efforts to fight the illegal gun trade. Perhaps the person who sold the gun to Radcliffe Haughton—the man who violated his restraining order to open fire at the nail salon where his estranged wife worked—knew that the man was stalking his wife, but how to prove that? Unless a prosecutor could prove the seller actually knew he was handing a weapon over to a felon, he broke no laws.

"That's a very, very high bar," the Third Way report says. "In fact, it is such a high bar that in a typical year, a person is only slightly more likely to be prosecuted for selling a gun to a prohibited person than they are to be attacked by an alligator."

The comparison might be amusing, but the problem it addresses is dead serious. Every single day, gun trafficking puts deadly weapons into the hands of criminals, and there are virtually no effective laws on the books to discourage the practice.

Another difference between drug dealing and gun trafficking is that the latter diverts the guns from legitimate (buying guns from a licensed dealer with a background check) to illegitimate (selling these same guns to people you suspect would fail a background check) commerce. The goal of fighting gun trafficking is to prevent that diversion from occurring—to keep guns out of the hands of dangerous people.

Until we can change our federal laws to safeguard people from back-alley transactions, we're happy to see states working hard to curtail gun trafficking. Seventeen states and the District of Columbia require a state-level dealer's license for all gun transactions, which is one effective way to reduce these unregulated gun sales.

*   *   *

Another way that guns get into the hands of the wrong people is through straw purchases, which usually take place through licensed dealers.

The majority of gun dealers in America are on the level. They follow the rules and try not to sell guns to straw purchasers, or people who are planning to pass the gun along to someone who wouldn't have been able to pass a background check.

But while most are honest and have a financial stake in selling their wares to responsible citizens, some licensed dealers do knowingly sell guns to criminals, for the simple reason that they *can*. Very few get caught, and when they do, the penalties are light. Consequences of breaking this particular law are so minimal that it's routinely flouted.

This has to change. Congress must pass a strong federal statute to combat gun trafficking and stiffen penalties for straw purchasing, so that anyone convicted of buying a firearm for another person will serve a significant sentence. We need to strengthen deterrents to these transactions, since right now there are almost none.

But the straw-purchasing controversy is another example of the NRA's perverse resistance to all reason or compromise: while claiming to support cracking down on straw purchases, the NRA aggressively fought to defeat Senate proposals that would've made straw purchasing punishable by up to twenty-five years in prison.

Congress also needs to crack down on licensed dealers who knowingly sell weapons to people who commit crimes. ATF's gun traces showed that 1 percent of licensed dealers account for 57 percent of guns recovered in crimes. That's a pretty disturbing statistic.

Take Sandy Abrams, who owned Valley Gun in Baltimore, as a prime example. In 2003 federal agents declared Abrams's store a "serial violator" of federal gun laws and revoked its license because the gun shop "endangered the public by failing to account for hundreds of weapons."

How did the NRA respond? It reelected Abrams to its board of directors.

In Milwaukee, federal agents traced guns from Badger Guns and Ammo to weapons that were later used in crimes. In 1999 the ATF released information showing that Badger led the nation in selling guns later tied to crimes. In response, Badger quit selling cheap handguns known as Saturday night specials. With that one change in practice, local police recovered 71 percent fewer new Saturday night specials used in crimes, according to Daniel Webster, director of the Johns Hopkins Center for Gun Policy and Research.

So we know enforcement and tracing illegally sold guns can make a dent in gun trafficking, but Congress and the NRA have weakened federal laws and undercut the ATF at every turn. How can the ATF monitor gun dealers and weed out ones like Sandy Abrams when a 1986 federal law says it can make unannounced inspections of gun shops no more than once a year? And even if federal or local police find evidence that dealers might be breaking the law, the penalties are almost nonexistent.

The good news is that many states have tightened regulation of gun sales. Massachusetts and Rhode Island mandate regular inspections of gun dealers. And in 2006, New York investigators fanned out to fifty-five gun dealers in seven states they suspected were the source of illegal guns used in New York crimes. Many of the guns came north from Georgia, South Carolina, Alabama, and Virginia along what's called the Iron Pipeline of illegal weapons. The investigators found evidence of twenty-seven dealers facilitating straw purchases. New York sued them. Nearly all of the dealers settled the suits by agreeing to change their practices and allow monitoring of their sales.

We know that enforcement can help stop bad dealers. We also know that the NRA has tried to hamper these efforts. In 2005 the NRA backed the Protection of Lawful Commerce in Arms Act, which protects manufacturers and gun dealers from being sued if guns they sold are later used in crimes, unless they "knowingly" sold them to straw buyers. Despite this hurdle, New York was able to make that case in its lawsuits.

Severing the Iron Pipeline is essential to keeping guns out of the wrong hands. Rather than weakening the ATF and cutting off its funding (which has happened repeatedly thanks to the NRA), Congress and states should stiffen laws against illegal firearm transactions—measures that the NRA also claims to support. Criminals convicted of operating gunrunning organizations should face felonies and serious jail time.

Congress also needs to treat the ATF and its agents as allies in keeping Americans safe from gun violence, rather than a pariah agency filled with LaPierre's nonexistent "jackbooted government thugs" out to get God-fearing Americans. The ATF deserves more funding and greater authority and stability—the agency is one of the most important tools we have in the fight against gun trafficking. Congress should also make it easier to approve an ATF director. Thanks in large part to opposition from the NRA, the bureau did not have a permanent director from 2006 until the Senate finally confirmed B. Todd Jones in July 2013.

Jones's confirmation was an important step in the right direction, but even so, as it currently stands, the ATF can't do its job efficiently. And thanks to constant interventions from the NRA, there aren't nearly enough penalties or provisions in place to ensure that only law-abiding citizens with no history of dangerous mental illness are the ones in possession of guns.

The way our current system is set up, anyone who wants a gun—whether convicted of a crime, or the subject of a restraining order, or with a known mental illness—can get one, without that much effort.

This has got to change.

＊　　＊　　＊

As Gabby and I studied the issue, we kept circling back to the same root problem over and over again: background checks. There were just too many ways of getting around the simple public-safety measures put in place to make sure that only qualified buyers could purchase guns. If we could get rid of the loopholes that make it easy for criminals and people suffering from dangerous mental illness to buy guns without submitting to a background check, we could go a long way toward keeping dangerous weapons out of the hands of the people least capable of handling them responsibly.

CHAPTER TEN

GUNS DON'T KILL PEOPLE. PEOPLE KILL PEOPLE.

O ne morning in March 2013, I left our house in Tucson and drove to a nearby gun store. I was in the market for a .45 semiautomatic pistol. I also wanted to demonstrate that our background-check system works quickly and efficiently.

After examining the gun-shop counter, I quickly settled on a SIG Sauer .45. It's a high-quality pistol from a European company that's manufactured in New Hampshire. I handed the clerk my driver's license, the only document required, and filled out a form.

Here are some of the questions on the Firearms Transaction Record, Form 4473, required for anyone buying a weapon from a federally licensed firearms dealer:

Was I under indictment for a felony? No.

Had I been convicted of a felony? No.

Was I a fugitive? Been adjudicated mentally deficient? Subject to a domestic-violence restraining order? Convicted of a misdemeanor in a domestic-violence matter? Dishonorably discharged? No to all of the above.

The store sent my name and responses to the FBI through the National Instant Criminal Background Check System (NICS).

"Can I get a couple boxes of nine-millimeter and forty-five-caliber ammo?" I asked.

Five minutes and thirty-six seconds after beginning to fill out the form, I left with my new pistol and the ammunition.

Why not make everyone who wants to buy a gun in America fill out these forms and answer these basic questions? Why not require everyone to pass a NICS background check, which takes less than ten minutes? It's clear to me—and to 93 percent of US households that have gun owners—that it makes common sense for anyone who wants to buy a gun to undertake a background check, just like the one I passed.

When Gabby and I founded Americans for Responsible Solutions, one of our first goals was expanding background checks to close the private-sale loophole. And the more we learned about gun violence in this country, the more emphasis we placed on this essential measure.

Our proposals about background checks are neither radical nor unreasonable. Right now in the US, it's harder to buy a box of Sudafed than it is to buy a lethal weapon. That is not okay. Expanding background checks is absolutely crucial to making our country safer from gun violence.

Background checks are quick, easy, and painless. So why doesn't every gun buyer in this country submit to one? According to a 1997 analysis by the National Institute of Justice, about 40 percent of all firearm sales did not transfer through a licensed dealer that requires a background check. There are no current figures, because no-check transactions are by their very nature invisible and Congress has barred the ATF from making gun-tracing data public. The actual number of firearms sold without a background check could be higher or lower than 40 percent.

Firearm transactions from non-licensed gun dealers at gun shows, in homes, out of cars, or over the Internet on sites like Armslist are all considered "private sales." Private sales are often the source of weapons that get into the hands of criminals, the dangerously mentally ill, or spouses bent on harming their partners. Will the next mass shooter buy his choice of lethal weapon at a gun show? It certainly wouldn't be that difficult.

Though he claims to favor fixing the mental health system that lets too many people like Jared Loughner slip through the cracks, the NRA's Wayne LaPierre would argue that Loughner, if denied a gun legally, could simply have gone to the "black market" and gotten a gun anyway.

Well, I'd like to invite Mr. LaPierre to Tucson, Arizona, and have him show me exactly where this black market is located. Loughner, Virginia Tech shooter Seung-Hui Cho, and James Holmes, the killer in Aurora, were not career criminals (which are, incidentally, another type of gun buyer that laws should make more of an effort to address). These men were isolated, shut-off individuals without great social connections or insider knowledge.

If the background-check system could have included adjudicated mental health histories for the men and the gun-show and Internet loopholes had been closed, it's likely that these mass shooters wouldn't have had the first clue of where to buy illegal guns—that is to say, finding that elusive "black market" wouldn't be so easy for most people, including Wayne LaPierre and myself.

And what about the guns used in the 1999 Columbine High massacre? The shooters—Eric Harris and Dylan Klebold—were both seventeen and knew they were too young to buy a gun. Klebold's friend Robyn Anderson was eighteen, so they asked her to buy weapons for them as a "straw buyer." She was too scared to fill out the required NICS form at a registered gun dealer, so they convinced her to buy one at the Tanner Gun Show in Adams County, Colorado, where she wouldn't have to fill anything out.

She bought guns that the two teenagers used to slaughter their students and teachers. If she had been required to fill out the form at the Tanner Gun Show to complete the purchase, maybe she would have refused their request. Would Eric Harris and Dylan Klebold have known where to find Wayne LaPierre's "black market"? I doubt it.

* * *

I won't deny that the NICS system has flaws: not all states report consistently, and people aren't prosecuted nearly enough for attempting to buy a gun when they're barred from doing so. Right now, in the majority of cases, the only penalty is that the person who fails the background check doesn't get the gun.

Even so, the background-check system functions well through federally licensed firearms dealers. Licensed gun dealers are not hard to find. They have set up shop everywhere from small towns to suburban strip malls. Nearly sixty thousand licensed retail gun dealers are open for business; that's nearly twice the number of post offices in this country.

So why is it that an estimated 40 percent of gun sales are completed with no background checks at all? Well, because there are so many convenient ways around them.

Under the Gun Control Act of 1968, federal law defined private sellers as anyone who sold no more than four firearms per year. But the 1986 Firearm Owners Protection Act, crafted and passed with help from the NRA, lifted that restriction. It loosely defined private sellers as people who do not rely on gun sales as the principal way of obtaining their livelihood. The effect of this vague language is that anyone can sell as many guns as they want in private sales, without checking the background of the buyer. And law enforcement has little ability to determine who is and who isn't breaking the law.

As I said before, this is not okay. We would all be safer if everyone who bought a gun passed a background check.

A vast majority of Americans agree. Republican pollster Frank Luntz in 2012 asked US gun owners if they supported criminal background checks for all gun sales. He found that 87 percent approved, including 74 percent of NRA members.

A *New York Times*/CBS poll in January 2013 concluded that 92 percent of all households—and 93 percent of gun-owning households—agree that if you're going to possess a gun, you should be able to pass a background check. A high level of support endures to this day all over the country, across most demographics.

As I proved when I bought the SIG Sauer .45, passing a background check is fast and efficient for law-abiding citizens. When I filled out the form and presented my driver's license, my name was checked against federal criminal records and reports submitted to NICS by states on a voluntary basis. The Justice Department reports that the National Instant Background Checks System, managed by the FBI, is "instantaneous" and completes 90 percent of background checks in a matter of minutes. By far, most Americans pass.

But some do not—and for very good reason. Between 1994 and 2009, NICS blocked about two million permit applications and gun sales to people who were prohibited by law from possessing guns: they include felons and people who have a warrant out for their arrest, have used drugs within the past year, were ruled mentally incompetent by a judge, are living in the US illegally, or have a domestic-violence conviction or a domestic-violence-related restraining order against them.

The NICS system works. But it is in no way "universal." If as many as 40 percent of gun sales roll right through the gaping private-sale loophole, let's close it.

*　　*　　*

Right now there are just too many ways for criminals to buy guns, without consequences for either the buyer or seller. With sites like Armslist, the Web provides a whole new bazaar for background-check-free gun exchanges, with background checks conducted on in-state but not interstate sales and no real rhyme or reason to the system.

New York state police investigated online gun sales in 2011 and found more than twenty-five thousand guns for sale on just ten sites. Under current law the precise volume of sales is unknowable, because many of these transfers create no record.

"Every day," the undercover investigators found, "firearms transactions are conducted on thousands of websites among largely anonymous actors. Criminal buyers who once had to purchase in person can now prowl hundreds of thousands of listings to find unscrupulous sellers."

New York State investigators found that 62 percent of private gun sellers agreed to sell a weapon to a buyer who said he or she most likely could not pass a background check. They concluded: "The private sale loophole and the private-sector failures that enable too many unscrupulous individuals to sell guns online, and too many dangerous people to buy them, should be reformed."

The *New York Times* in 2013 investigated the buying and selling of weapons on Armslist. It found that "private parties," which do not require background checks, posted 94 percent of the ads. Among the traders, the *Times* found Gerard Toolin, a South Carolina man "who is a fugitive from the Rhode Island police and has two outstanding felony warrants as well as a misdemeanor warrant." Based on that record, Toolin cannot own guns. But on Armslist he was looking to buy an AK-47 assault rifle and trying to trade a Marlin rifle. Toolin posted photos of guns he had already purchased, including an AK-47. Gun sales on the Internet are essentially a free-for-all, and this is a problem.

* * *

Gun shows are another place where people sure to fail NICS background checks can go for their choice of weaponry. Closing the so-called "gun show loophole" is essential for keeping Americans safe from gun violence.

New York State has taken some important steps to ensure that weapons sold at gun shows don't get into the wrong hands. Attorney General Eric Schneiderman described the process to Gabby and me in detail. As part of the 2011 investigation, he sent agents to purchase weapons at three gun shows. New York State has required background checks at gun shows since 2000, but these investigators were able to buy eleven guns, including semiautomatics, from ten private sellers without passing background checks. The ten sellers were arrested. Even when laws are in place, there are too many ways around them.

Schneiderman then met with operators of the largest number of gun shows in the state. They agreed to procedures that would track all guns brought into a show by private sellers. Each weapon is tagged so that operators could track sales and background checks. Private sellers have to account for every gun they bring to the show; if they sell a weapon, they have to produce paperwork to prove that the buyer passed a background check, and the buyer has to show proof that he passed a check before leaving the show with his purchase.

After Schneiderman described New York's approach, Gabby and I thought it could serve as a model for other states. We traveled to Saratoga Springs, New York, in the fall of 2013, toured a gun show with Schneiderman, and spoke with gun dealers who said the new system was working well. Some leaders of the state's NRA had also gotten on board with the provisions, and even helped draft them. The new provisions in New York State proved that firearm commerce could thrive at gun shows that tracked guns in and out of the building and enforced background checks.

For Internet and other private sales, buyers could complete background checks online by applying through a portal in the NICS system. If we have the technology for Americans to apply through secure systems online for bank loans to buy a house, certainly we can create one for those who want to buy guns.

If nine out of ten Americans support these simple measures, what's stopping our lawmakers from acting on the will of their constituents?

Forget all the loopholes and exceptions. Anyone who

wants to buy a gun should do as I did and fill out a Form 4473, just as they would do at a licensed dealer.

Let's say you're selling a deer rifle or a handgun at a gun show. Just because Congress doesn't require a background check, you should still be a responsible gun owner and make sure that your gun is going into safe hands. You could ask the buyer to fill out a Form 4473. If you don't have the ability to conduct a background check yourself, you can find a federally licensed firearm dealer at a gun show who can then submit the form to NICS.

Gabby and I are working hard to make background checks for all a reality in America. The process would take just a few short minutes, and it could save untold numbers of lives.

CHAPTER ELEVEN

LONG ODDS

Two weeks after we launched Americans for Responsible Solutions, Vermont Senator Patrick Leahy asked Gabby and me to testify before the Judiciary Committee's initial hearing about gun violence.

It was an extraordinary opportunity to jump into the middle of this looming debate, but we were very new at this. Our organization was in its infancy. Our small staff was still hunting for office space. Gabby and I were gradually getting used to our new roles. I knew Gabby could pull it off, but I wasn't sure if I was ready to testify before the United States Senate.

In the wake of the Newtown massacre, opposing sides of the gun-violence debate had staked out their positions in the media and in Washington. The NRA and its allies on Capitol Hill had declared their opposition to any efforts to pass new laws about guns, despite polls showing that the majority of Americans favored stronger gun legislation, especially expanded background checks.

The Judiciary Committee hearing would be the first time the country would have the chance to witness a live, official debate on gun violence—not just since Newtown, but in

191

years. It would also serve as the opening volley for the bitter battle over new federal gun laws.

When Chairman Leahy gaveled the committee hearing to order on January 30, 2013, Gabby would be speaking on the public record, before a national audience, and her testimony would be preserved in the *Congressional Record*. The last time she had spoken in that official capacity was two years before, on January 6, 2011, when she took the House floor to suggest lawmakers cut their pay to reduce the deficit, on the same day she read the First Amendment.

If Gabby's appearance at the Democratic National Convention was any indication, she was more than capable of dazzling the Judiciary Committee. On September 6, 2012, Gabby had surprised the convention by showing up to deliver the pledge of allegiance. She walked across the stage with her friend, Congresswoman Debbie Wasserman Schultz, chairwoman of the DNC. No cane, no brace for her right arm. From the moment she took her first steps under the lights, Gabby beamed. They stopped to face the audience, already cheering "Gabby!"

Gabby took a deep breath. She had to hold her right arm against her heart with her good left hand.

"I," Debbie started, and Gabby took it from there.

Not only did she recite the pledge well, she looked directly at the conventioneers and delivered the pledge with perfect pitch and gusto.

"AND to the republic."

"FOR which it stands."

"ONE nation."

"UNDER God."

"INDIVISIBLE . . ."

For a woman who battled aphasia every day, it was a superb performance. In her irrepressible fashion, she made it a special moment. She waved as she walked off the stage. She managed to transform her limp into a swinging stroll.

But testifying before the Senate Judiciary Committee would present a different type of challenge. Some of the committee members were staunch NRA allies, reflexively opposed to our push for expanded background checks and some sensible legislation. We knew they'd be deferential and respectful toward Gabby, but still—were we ready to take center stage?

Together with our ARS staff, we debated whether the moment was right for Gabby, for me, and for our young organization. It would be my first-ever testimony before a congressional committee, and I have to admit I was a little nervous. Surely there would be more hearings in the months to come, when we would be better prepared? Pia Carusone, often the voice of caution, decided it for us.

"This is going to be a big, big day," she said. "Let's do it."

Gabby was all in.

* * *

On Friday, January 25, I phoned Fabi Kruse, Gabby's speech therapist.

"Fabi," I asked, "what are you doing next week?"

As soon as we moved back to Tucson in August, we searched for the best speech therapist in town and soon found Fabi Kruse. She had worked in the field for twenty years. She was not only an expert in speech therapy, but she specialized in treating aphasia, the lasting condition from Gabby's traumatic brain injury. Fabi had been treating aphasia patients for a decade. Beginning in August, she came to our house three times a week for two-hour sessions with Gabby. She became part of the family.

"Busy week," she said. "Why?"

193

"Gabby is scheduled to testify before the Senate Judiciary Committee in Washington on January 30," I said. "She's writing a short statement that she will have to deliver in a high-pressure situation. Will the two of you have enough time to prepare?"

When Fabi and Gabby first started working together, they sometimes took a couple of weeks to prepare for a public appearance. Polishing Gabby's delivery of the pledge of allegiance before the DNC came easily. She had full command of the words and the melody. In November 2012 the American Speech Language and Hearing Association asked Gabby to deliver some remarks. With Fabi's guidance, Gabby wrote a five-line speech and perfected it over the course of weeks of therapy.

This time they had less than a week.

"I can do it," Gabby said.

After we committed to establishing Americans for Responsible Solutions, Gabby's therapy had taken a new direction. Learning about the issues, working on language, and preparing to speak provided the perfect combination of focused therapy with a goal. Gabby understood the complexity of speaking about gun violence, and grappling with the intricacies of background checks and gun-trafficking laws motivated her to work even harder. Gabby always loved to work toward goals. Returning to the public stage was an essential part of her recovery.

Fabi saw Gabby's command of the language improve every session. "You cannot imagine how hard she works," Fabi said to me.

I didn't have to imagine. Gabby takes her iPad to bed many nights to practice reading, writing, and talking. I often fall asleep to the sound of my wife's voice.

* * *

Gabby worked with Pia and her staff to draft remarks to the Judiciary Committee. It was a short speech, about fifteen lines.

Then they got down to the hard work of turning a brief speech into powerful oratory.

The first time through, on January 25, Gabby couldn't articulate many of the lines very accurately. Fabi read the speech a few times. Gabby watched her lips. Gabby tried to join in.

"Hey, hey," Fabi said. "Listen first."

Over the next few days, the two of them practiced tirelessly. If Gabby had trouble with a word, she would edit it out.

Gabby struggled with the first line: "Thank you for inviting me here today." She kept dropping "me." After a day, she had it down.

The original speech read: "Speaking is difficult, but I want you to hear from me because I know how important this is."

Fabi and Gabby simplified it to: "Speaking is difficult, but I need to say something important."

Clearer and better.

The draft read: "Too many people are dying. Too many children."

Gabby replaced "people" with "children" and read it in both lines, over and over. People struggling with aphasia often get stuck on certain words or default phrases. Gabby was stuck on *children*.

The day before we flew to Washington, DC, Gabby recited the speech with six or seven glitches. She and Fabi worked on the plane to DC. By the time we landed Gabby had it down to two.

Just twenty-two days after the birth of Americans for Responsible Solutions, we were driving the national debate on gun violence. Gabby was ready to take on the Judiciary Committee—and the world.

* * *

But was *I* ready? I was scheduled to testify before a committee packed with gun-rights proponents, on a panel that included Wayne LaPierre. I felt comfortable speaking in public about my life and work as an astronaut. This would be my first time testifying, debating, and facing questions about public policy issues around gun violence that I was just beginning to grasp. I was stepping out of my comfort zone. I had been practicing, but not as much as Gabby. She worked on her delivery when we arrived at the hotel and the next morning, too.

Then it was time to take the ride to the Senate office building on Capitol Hill.

"How are you feeling?" I asked on the hotel elevator.

"Pretty good," Gabby responded.

"Ready for this?"

She nodded.

Senator Leahy greeted us as we got off the elevator down the hall from the committee room. The Judiciary Committee chairman is a tall, affable former prosecutor who had been representing his home state of Vermont in the Senate since 1975. He represents a rural state and defends the rights of gun owners, but he had also supported a ban on assault weapons and was for universal background checks. He had introduced his own bill that would give law enforcement more tools to investigate gun trafficking and straw purchasers.

"Thank you, Gabby," Leahy said. "It's great having you here."

Jeff Flake walked past Leahy and wrapped Gabby in his arms. Jeff, the newly elected senator from Arizona, was an old friend.

"Good to see you," Jeff said.

"Yes, yes, yes," Gabby said, "good to see you, too."

Gabby and Jeff had been close for years as they rose through Arizona's political ranks. They had served in Congress together during Gabby's three terms and had forged an unlikely political alliance. Of course, they did share some similarities: she was a Democrat who was not afraid to cross lines and support conservative issues; Flake was a Republican who sometimes sought the middle ground, crossing over on immigration votes while he was in the House. And even when Gabby disagreed with Jeff on a political issue, she thought he was a genuinely good person.

Gabby and Jeff also shared a deep pride in their Arizona heritage: she was a third-generation Arizonan, while his family had been in the state five generations. On the day she was shot, Jeff jumped into his car and drove two and a half hours from Phoenix to the Tucson hospital where she was undergoing surgery. He didn't announce his arrival or expect any special reception. He just sat alone in the waiting room, quietly awaiting reports and praying for her recovery. Like I said: a genuinely good person.

Over the years I had become friends with Jeff, too. We had even talked about going hunting together for mountain lion. Given his commonsense approach to government and his friendship with Gabby, we saw him as a potential ally on gun violence.

The warm greeting between Gabby and Jeff was a nice

moment, but we wondered where he would come down in the gun-violence debate.

* * *

Jeff Flake was the newest member of the powerful Senate Judiciary Committee. Its eighteen members have broad jurisdiction over federal law, from immigration to Internet privacy, from confirming federal judges to debating changes to federal gun laws. If we hoped to change laws on background checks or gun trafficking, we would have to start here.

The committee members were a perfect reflection of our imperfect political system that was too easily gummed up by partisan differences.

Among the Democrats were California's Dianne Feinstein, New York's Chuck Schumer, Dick Durbin of Illinois, and Richard Blumenthal of Connecticut. They had been supportive of gun-law reform. Feinstein had championed the 1994 assault-weapons ban and was planning to reintroduce a similar measure. Chairman Leahy was thoughtful and sympathetic to laws that might cut down gun violence. We hoped the other five Democrats—Amy Klobuchar and Al Franken from Minnesota, Delaware's Chris Coons, Sheldon Whitehouse from Rhode Island, and Hawaii's Mazie Hirono—would be willing to work with us.

The committee had a confirmed conservative core, too, but at the time we still thought we might be able to put a deal together. We even believed that the NRA might join us in supporting expanded background checks. Why wouldn't they? Wayne LaPierre had spoken forcefully in favor of background checks as recently as 1999 when he said, "No loopholes anywhere, for anyone." Fourteen years later, was there a possibility that LaPierre would return to this earlier sensible position—and, more importantly, authorize the members of Congress he controls to follow his lead?

Of course I always knew it would be an uphill battle. The committee's eight Republicans were likely to oppose any new restrictions on gun ownership. Chuck Grassley from Iowa, the highest-ranking Republican, was a strong conservative, especially when it came to gun rights. Utah's Orrin Hatch, Jeff Sessions from Alabama, and Utah's Mike Lee would also probably not be amenable to a compromise, even though the vast majority of the country supported the measure. Lindsey Graham of South Carolina faced reelection and was tacking right. Texas Republican Ted Cruz, a darling of the Tea Party and the NRA, was the most unapologetic right-wing favorite on the committee.

If we wanted to strengthen the federal government's ability to protect Americans from gun violence, we had to start with the Senate. It had passed a ban on cheap handguns in 1972. The 1994 assault-weapons ban originated in the Senate. As we prepared to testify, we knew we needed every vote we could get to strengthen background checks.

Hailing from the middle ground—where we mirrored the views of most Americans—Gabby and I hoped to convince the committee's moderates to consider our proposals to stem gun violence.

But how would the NRA weigh in?

* * *

Chairman Leahy gaveled the hearing to order shortly after ten A.M. Before the members read their statements, Leahy said Gabby would lead off the session.

We had made our way to the long testimony table, facing the dais and the senators. It took us a while. People stopped

Gabby along the way. Cameras flashed. Gabby took her seat, with me to her left. She settled in, looked down at the hand-written speech on lined paper. She thanked the senators for inviting her. Then she slowly but surely started to speak:

"This is an important conversation.

"For our children. For our communities.

"For Democrats and Republicans.

"Speaking is difficult, but I need to say something important."

Gabby was speaking in her deliberate, halting cadence. In that setting, her short speech was all the more powerful and affecting. Gabby's struggle with each word became everyone's struggle. The whole country was pulling for her.

The room was packed, the flashbulbs clicking. As she began to speak, I watched senators wiping tears from their eyes. It was a tremendously emotional moment that I will remember for the rest of my life.

"Too many children are dying," she said. "Too many children."

Fabi, sitting in the back of the hearing room, knew the script read "Too many people are dying," but Gabby's repeating "children" actually packed more punch. Then Gabby hit her stride.

"We must do SOMETHING!" she said, looking straight at the senators and lifting up in her seat for emphasis.

"It will be hard," emphasis on *hard*.

"But the time is NOW," she said.

Now she was shooting her look right at the committee.

"You must act!

"Be bold!

"Be courageous!" she said. "Americans are counting on you."

She thanked the committee and swung her left hand across her chest as if to say: I did it, and you better have listened.

Fabi Kruse was in awe of Gabby's ability to strike just the right tone, under the pressure and glare of the moment. Pia Carusone and Peter Ambler, sitting right behind us, were not shocked. Her staff knew that Gabby had never lost her innate instinct to get her points across when it counted using every tool she could muster, and she still had plenty.

* * *

After the senators read their statements, it was my turn to testify. I was on a panel that included Baltimore County police chief Jim Johnson, NRA leader Wayne LaPierre, Gayle Trotter with the Independent Women's Forum, and constitutional law professor David Kopel.

Gabby evoked the heart of our movement, and my job was delivering the detail. I started by congratulating "Gabby's friend and much respected former colleague, Jeff Flake, on his new role as Arizona's junior senator."

I was probably a lot more nervous than Gabby. This whole experience was just totally new for me. Sure, I got a few butterflies in my stomach before launching at night from the deck of an aircraft carrier or rocketing into space, but testifying before a Senate committee was a whole different ball game. But if Gabby had done it, so could I.

I began by making clear to the committee that Gabby and I consider ourselves moderates—and that we are gun owners—who were jolted by the Newtown shootings: "We are simply two reasonable Americans who have said, 'Enough.'"

I described the Tucson shooting in a few sentences.

"There isn't a single action or law that could have elegantly prevented the Tucson shooting from being written into the history books," I said. "Gabby is one of roughly one hundred thousand victims of gun violence in America every year. Behind every victim lays a matrix of failure and inadequacy—in our families, communities, and values; in our society's approach to poverty, violence, and mental illness; and, yes, in our politics and in our gun laws.

"One of our messages is simple: the breadth and complexity of gun violence is great—but it is not an excuse for inaction."

Gabby and I believe "wholly and completely in the Second Amendment," I told the senators, and added: "Our rights are paramount. But our responsibilities are serious. And as a nation we are not taking responsibility for the gun rights our founders conferred upon us."

I urged the senators to fix background checks, to remove limitations on collecting data and conducting research on gun violence, to toughen federal gun-trafficking laws, and to "have a careful and civil conversation about the lethality of the firearms we permit to be legally bought and sold in this country."

Baltimore County police chief Johnson, in dress-blue uniform hung with medals, pleaded for stronger background checks, too. Like many law-enforcement officers, he rightfully saw the proliferation of illegal guns as a threat to police officers. The NRA's policy of advocating gun ownership for all, with absolutely no commonsense restrictions whatsoever, increasingly struck many officers as irresponsible and potentially dangerous.

Chief Johnson made the case for closing the private-sale loophole. "Allowing forty percent of those acquiring guns to bypass background checks is like allowing forty percent of airline passengers to board a plane without going through airport security," he told the committee.

Delaware Senator Chris Coons asked Wayne LaPierre for his thoughts on a universal background check. The NRA chief said it "ends up being a universal federal nightmare imposed upon law-abiding people all over this country" and would be a "huge waste of resources."

Coons put the question to Chief Johnson: would a universal background check combined with aggressive enforcement of illegal transfers make a difference? Johnson said he would have to "respectfully disagree with Wayne" and added, "Public safety, police, we are ready, we are unified on this issue, that a universal background check will make our society a safer place, will make my police officers safer. It's absolutely essential."

Two exchanges stood out for me.

A few Republican senators parroted the NRA line that arming more citizens would make the country safer, that a good guy with a gun was the answer to gun violence.

I had to respond to that. "I've been shot at dozens of times," I said. "I would suspect that not many members of this panel, or even in this room, for that matter, have been in any kind of a firefight. It is—it is chaos. I think there are really some very effective things we can do. And one is, Senator, the background check. Let's make it difficult for the criminals, the terrorists, and the mentally ill to get a gun."

The second exchange involved something Senator Charles Grassley said in his opening remarks. I was a bit surprised to hear him describe the federal government as potentially "tyrannical," a word you might expect to hear from members of the NRA fringe. Later in the hearing, Illinois Democrat Dick Durbin picked up on the "tyranny" matter and asked

Wayne LaPierre if he subscribed to the notion that Americans might need to take up arms against the government, as some NRA members believe. LaPierre sidestepped the question but said many feel "abandoned by the government" and arm themselves for "fundamental human survival."

Durbin asked Chief Johnson how he felt about those in the NRA who believe the Second Amendment gives American citizens "the firepower to fight back against you—against our government. So how do you conduct your business in enforcing the law not knowing what is behind that door?"

"I find it to be scary," the chief responded, "creepy, and simply just not based on logic."

*   *   *

About three hours into the hearing, I bolted down the hall for a bathroom break. David Kopel arrived seconds later. Kopel had been testifying along with me at the hearing, but he and I had a different take on gun violence. Through his books, articles, and legal arguments, Kopel had become a prominent voice against any attempt at limiting the right to bear arms. An associate policy analyst with the libertarian Cato Institute and adjunct professor at Denver University's Strum College of Law, he told senators that neither expanded background checks nor a ban on assault weapons would have any effect on crime or mass murders.

In the bathroom, I took the opportunity to ask him a question.

"If you had to choose between two guns for self-protection—a fully automatic tommy gun or an AR-15—which would you pick?" I asked. The tommy gun had been regulated under the 1934 firearms act. But anyone who knows about guns will tell you the AR-15 is the better weapon, certainly more accurate and lethal.

"I don't know," he responded. "I don't understand those kinds of details."

It turns out Kopel had been plenty well versed in the differences between automatic and semiautomatic weapons to write about them for the *Wall Street Journal* right after the Newtown slaughter. In an article, Kopel had dived into the details of guns and gun laws and described the AR-15: "unlike automatics (machine guns), they fire only one bullet each time the trigger is pressed."

Kopel knows the "details" of guns and gun law. In his books, articles, and legal briefs, he has become one of the most strident critics of any restrictions on gun ownership. The NRA supports his work with generous grants.

Later, I found out that in 2011 the NRA Civil Rights Defense Fund gave Kopel a $108,000 research grant and a share of another grant for $55,000. On his website, Kopel mentions that he's an NRA member, but he doesn't list his financial ties to the NRA. He also conveniently neglected to bring up those ties in his Senate testimony.

Back at the Senate hearing, I knew that LaPierre and Kopel were aligned against us, but I didn't know at the time that LaPierre's organization had actually helped fund Kopel's research.

*   *   *

After four hours of debate and testimony, the committee was split along party lines. The Republicans, in general, sided with Wayne LaPierre and the NRA in opposing any major changes to federal gun laws; the Democrats spoke in favor of strengthening background checks, but support for a ban on assault weapons appeared to be weak.

Senator Flake went down the hall to visit Gabby as she watched the proceedings by video. Back on the dais, he devoted a large part of his statement to thanking Gabby and me for testifying and for "our dedication to this cause." In his remarks and questions, he stuck to mental health matters and avoided any discussion on background checks.

We took heart when New York Senator Charles Schumer said, "Universal background checks is a proven, effective step we can take to reduce gun violence, and I believe it has a good chance of passing." Senator Leahy promised to pass a bill through his committee so the full Senate could debate gun violence.

When Senator Leahy gaveled the Senate hearing to an end, I walked around the table and shook Wayne LaPierre's hand. He seemed surprised, certainly speechless. He didn't smile.

That afternoon President Obama invited us to the White House. We had a private meeting in the Oval Office—just the three of us. In the few minutes we spent together, the president hugged Gabby and congratulated her on her testimony. He promised to fight hard for universal background checks.

We left feeling hopeful, but we also had a better sense of the fight we faced. LaPierre and the NRA weren't going to surrender an inch of ground.

CHAPTER TWELVE

SENATE SHOWDOWN

In the second week of April 2013, the Senate returned from a two-week recess and hurtled toward a major vote on gun violence. Or rather, the Senate *lurched* toward a vote—as politicians, advocates, victims of gun violence, and lobbyists jockeyed for position.

The day of reckoning on the Senate floor had been taking shape for months. After Gabby and I testified in January, Judiciary Committee Chairman Patrick Leahy had proposed a package of gun-related bills. He held a series of hearings on gun trafficking, assault weapons, and background checks.

We kept track of the developments from Tucson and stayed in touch with senators along the way, thanks to our staff on the ground in Washington.

Families of the Newtown victims closely followed the legislation, too, and some showed up at Leahy's hearings. They were determined to turn their tragedy into stronger laws to prevent future gun violence. At one February 27 hearing on gun-control proposals, Neil Heslin recalled his son, Jesse McCord Lewis, the morning of the shooting.

"As Jesse was getting out of the truck, he leaned in and hugged me," Heslin said. He held up a portrait of his son and wept. "I can still feel that hug, and that pat on the back. He said, 'Everything's going to be okay, Dad, it's all going to be okay.' And it wasn't okay."

While Heslin and the Newtown families sitting behind him at the hearing supported many of the new legislative proposals, the NRA prepared to punish any senators who strayed from its dogma. Any movement toward more reasonable solutions would result in blacklisting.

By April 11, Majority Leader Harry Reid of Nevada prepared to call for votes on a wide variety of gun-violence measures, the most promising of which expanded the system of background checks to close most loopholes. Many Republicans adamantly opposed any change in gun laws and threatened a filibuster to stall action on legislation that came to the Senate floor.

This was too much for Erica Lafferty, daughter of Sandy Hook Elementary School Principal Dawn Hochsprung, whom Adam Lanza shot dead with his powerful rifle. Erica took to Twitter to contact fourteen Republican senators backing the filibuster. Texas Senator Ted Cruz, among the most opposed to proposed gun-law reform, called her back in response.

On MSNBC Lafferty said she asked Cruz during their call why he wasn't doing his job by simply debating the issue. "I asked him what would have happened if my mom chose not to do her job on December 14, because things would have turned out a lot different than they did," she said. Her mother had run into the hallway to confront the gunman when she heard shots. Lafferty said Cruz told her the proposed legislation wouldn't help prevent another massacre.

"I don't get what they're scared of," Lafferty said on the cable channel. "Mom wasn't scared in the hallways of Sandy Hook. You're an elected member of Congress. Stop being scared. Do your job. There's a ton of pieces to this puzzle, and background checks are the first part of that puzzle." .

* * *

The Senate had been circulating several proposals on background checks throughout the early months of 2013, but it wasn't until early April, when moderate senators from different parties came together, that a possibility with real potential emerged.

West Virginia Senator Joe Manchin is a strong supporter of gun rights and an NRA member, a lifelong hunter with an A rating from the organization. (In one of his most famous political ads, the burly Manchin had aimed his rifle and shot a cap-and-trade bill.) But Manchin had been profoundly affected by the tragedy at Sandy Hook, and he had been working on a background-check bill since January 2013.

The goal of Manchin's bill was specific and concrete: to close the gun-show and Internet loophole. It would extend the checks required by federally licensed firearms dealers to gun shows, Internet sales, classified-ad sales—any sale that is essentially commercial. Private sales or "transfers" between family members, neighbors, and friends would not require a background check.

To have a fighting chance at passing the bill, Manchin needed a Republican partner.

On March 28, Peter Ambler, who is in charge of Americans for Responsible Solutions' legislative advocacy and strategy, contacted Pennsylvania Republican Pat Toomey's staff. He explained Manchin's legislation and received an encouraging reply. Seeing common ground, Ambler and our other staffers informed Manchin's staff that Toomey was open to collaborating.

"They really ignited the fire," a senior Senate aide would later tell the *Washington Post*.

Though they came from different political parties, Manchin and Toomey were natural allies. Both were fiscal conservatives. Their states share a border, and they had worked together on energy issues. They trusted each other.

The Newtown bloodshed had shaken Toomey, too. He had asked aides to explore proposals to change gun laws in ways that might prevent another shooting rampage. Like Manchin, Toomey was close to the NRA. The group had given him an A rating and contributed heavily to his 2010 campaign. To inform his views on gun violence, Toomey had consulted the NRA, but he had also made some raw political calculations about the purple state he represented. Toomey concluded that Pennsylvanians would welcome his support of a stronger background-check law.

Manchin and Toomey met and talked in private. Their negotiations didn't leak to the press or their colleagues. Their staffs worked out language they both could accept. On Wednesday, April 10, the two senators went public with the Public Safety and Second Amendment Rights Protection Act.

The resulting proposal was not the work of extremists. Manchin-Toomey had a limited scope: all it did was extend the background-check provisions to gun shows and Internet sales, with ample exceptions. "As under current law," read a press release detailing the bill, "transfers between family, friends and neighbors do not require background checks. You can give or sell a gun to your brother, your neighbor, your co-worker without a background check. You can post a gun for sale on the cork bulletin board at your church or your job without a background check."

The bill also incentivized states to do a better job of entering criminal records into the background-check system to prevent people with known mental illnesses, like the Virginia Tech shooter, from purchasing firearms.

It's important to note that Manchin-Toomey included a specific ban on any sort of "national gun registry," the possibility of which had formed the centerpiece of the NRA's inflammatory rhetoric against background checks. Manchin-Toomey strengthened the penalties for attempting to create such a registry by increasing the charge from a misdemeanor to a felony, a measure taken to appease the very small minority in this country who genuinely worry about this issue.

And in certain aspects, the bill actually loosened restrictions on gun buying by expanding the interstate sales of guns, which were then limited to rifles and shotguns, to handguns as well.

"I am a parent and a grandfather," Manchin said in an emotional meeting with Newtown families, "and I had to do something." On a more political note, he said: "We're letting our country be governed and dictated by extremes."

Gabby and I were thrilled that ARS helped put the two together. The bill was a compromise we could support.

"What made the Giffords group successful," a senior Senate aide told the *Post*, "is that they are in the sweet spot that is not ideologically driven, but instead fact-driven. Their approach is to come from the middle which allows them to have credibility on both sides."

*   *   *

The Senate scheduled its votes on gun-violence measures on Wednesday, April 17. Gabby and I knew we had to be there. Senators were taking sides. We had been talking to a few by phone. Now it was time to make our case in person.

"We have a shot at this," I said to Gabby as we left home early Monday morning to board a flight to DC.

"Hard," she said. "But yes." Gabby wasn't naïve. She had a lot more experience in politics than I did, and she knew how unpredictable these votes could be. She also had the good sense to stay focused on the long game.

To get to sixty votes for the Manchin-Toomey bill, which would end debate and protect it from stalling tactics, we needed every Democrat in the room plus six Republicans. Under the Senate's complicated rules, a simple majority—51 to 49—would allow Republican opponents to add amendments as poison pills to weaken or kill the bill. It would open the process up to weeks of debate. We needed sixty.

*   *   *

We landed in Washington early Monday evening, both to take part in the debate and to honor Gabe Zimmerman, Gabby's staffer who had lost his life in the Tucson shooting.

That night we gathered with our staff and friends and Gabby's former congressional aides for a dinner to remember Gabe. It was a bittersweet affair. We told stories, laughed, and cried. Gabe's parents, Ross Zimmerman and Emily Nottingham, shared tales of young Gabe.

In January of 2012, we had dedicated the Gabe Zimmerman Davidson Canyon Trailhead at the trail's gateway southeast of Tucson. Gabe, who was thirty when Jared Loughner killed him, loved to hike and bike the trails around the city. He had worked hard on the measure to designate the Davidson Canyon Trail route as a National Scenic Trail. It was fitting that his name and his image welcomed people to the trail he loved so much.

Congress honored Gabe Zimmerman, too. Congresswoman Debbie Wasserman Schultz had introduced a bill to dedicate a meeting room in the Capitol Visitor Center in Gabe's honor. With the help of House Speaker John Boehner, the bill passed unanimously, and the dedication was scheduled for Tuesday, the day after our dinner for Gabe.

Dedicating the room to Gabe made history. It was the first space in the new visitor center to be dedicated to an individual. And it was the first room in the entire Capitol complex to be named in honor of a staff member. You can find statues and portraits and plaques commemorating politicians throughout the Capitol, congressional office buildings, and grounds. This would be the first to honor the staffers who labor tirelessly behind the scenes to help make laws and solve problems for constituents.

When Gabby arrived at Gabe's event Tuesday afternoon, staffers had already filled the spacious room. Minority Leader Nancy Pelosi, Congresswoman Wasserman Schultz, Senator Flake, and Congressman Ron Barber, who had succeeded Gabby in the House, were on hand to speak. Speaker Boehner choked up a bit as he welcomed the crowd.

"This isn't the space we use for pomp and ceremony," Boehner said. "People come here for meetings and gatherings, democratic rituals in their own right, the kind of assemblies Gabe planned and led throughout his career."

Gabe's career in Congress began in 2006 when Ron Barber made him his first hire in Gabby's Tucson office, as head of constituent services. "All of us wish we weren't here today," Barber said. "We wish Gabe were still with us. He led a life of such joy, passion, and curiosity."

Barber, who had directed Gabby's Tucson office, was by her side when Jared Loughner opened fire. Two bullets knocked Barber to the ground and nearly killed him. He recovered, and after Gabby resigned, Barber ran for and won Gabby's congressional seat, with her blessing. At the shooting, Barber recalled seeing Gabe at the back of the crowd and then by his side on the ground: after Gabe heard the shots, he had rushed to Gabby's side.

When Gabby and I took the microphone, I reminded everyone that Gabe was the only congressional staffer ever murdered in the line of duty. If Gabby could speak as well as she once could, I said, "she would keep you here all day long—"

"All day long," Gabby butted in. "All day."

"—talking about her friend Gabe," I finished.

I had looked into the Tucson shooting in detail.

"It was no surprise for me to learn that immediately after the shooting started, Gabe ran toward Gabby and other victims," I said, "toward the shooter and toward danger. Putting himself in service to others was Gabe's last act on earth."

Vice President Biden surprised us by showing up to honor Gabe. He comforted Gabe's family, made us laugh, and honored the staffers who make Congress function.

We lingered after the ceremony, feeling the warmth and collegiality of this moment. The dedication of Gabe's meeting room was a peaceful respite from the conflict over gun legislation that would come to a climax in the next twenty-four hours.

Congress could come together to honor Gabe Zimmerman, murdered by a madman who should never have had access to a firearm. Could it honor him with laws that might prevent the next mass murder?

* * *

I ran into Arizona Senator Jeff Flake in the hallway before the dedication of Gabe's meeting room.

SENATE SHOWDOWN

"Did you get my text?" I asked.

He took out his phone to check.

First thing that morning, I had attended the *Christian Science Monitor*'s regular breakfast for journalists and people in the news. The reporters and editors wanted my take on the series of votes on gun legislation, scheduled for Wednesday.

"A lot of senators are looking for a reason to just get to 'no,' " I told the reporters and editors. "I experienced that personally last night when shown the Facebook posting of Senator Jeff Flake, Gabby's good friend. He posted that he intends to vote 'no' on this legislation."

When one of the reporters asked if I would back a challenger to Flake's reelection, I hesitated.

I said, "You know, friendship is one thing. Saving people's lives, especially first graders', is another thing."

I had such complicated feelings about our old friend that morning.

Jeff had been there when we needed him. He had come to visit Gabby in the hospital after the Tucson shooting, and I will never forget the concern on his face in the waiting room that day. He had stayed in close touch with us in the difficult months that followed, regularly calling me and Pia to offer us much-needed reassurance and support. Jeff had sat by my wife's side when she attended the 2013 State of the Union, and I would never forget his friendship and loyalty to Gabby.

But how he voted on this first piece of legislation that could actually make a dent in gun violence mattered. If Jeff Flake, a moderate Republican senator, supported a gun-violence-prevention measure that the majority of his constituents backed, then others in his position might also be encouraged to cross the line.

After the *Christian Science Monitor* breakfast, I had sent Jeff

215

a text alerting him of my comments. I didn't want him to read them first in the media. As we stood in the hallway, he read my text and shook his head.

"What do we have to do to get you to 'yes'?" I asked him. We understood exactly what Jeff was up against, but Gabby and I both believed that Manchin-Toomey was a bill worth fighting for.

Jeff said he had problems with the bill's wording, rather than the intent. We had a productive discussion about items that seemed small and solvable, and in spite of it all, I held out hope that we could persuade Jeff and his colleagues to back Manchin-Toomey.

We knew how formidable an opponent the NRA could be, but maybe this time common sense would win out over intimidation.

* * *

In the car from Capitol Hill back to our downtown hotel, I got on the phone with Republican Senator Dan Coats from Indiana.

"What can I do to get you to change your vote?" I asked, knowing he was a long shot.

Coats had been a senator from 1989 to 1999, then retired and ran again in 2010. In his first term, he had voted for the Brady Bill and the 1994 ban on assault weapons. The votes prompted the NRA to oppose his candidacy.

This time around, he had voted for the filibuster. "I'm not going to support something that would violate the Second Amendment," Coats had said.

We were desperate for Republican votes, but Coats told me that morning that he was more likely to get behind another legislative approach.

Next up was North Dakota Senator Heidi Heitkamp, who we hoped might be a solid "maybe." She was a freshman Democrat, so new to the Senate that she was still camped out in a temporary office when I spoke with her. She told me that calls and e-mails from her constituents were running around six to one against her supporting the expanded background-checks legislation. North Dakota has a high number of gun owners and low rates of gun violence.

"It's just really tough, Mark," I remember her saying.

In other words: another no.

Later, as we left, Gabby and I wondered what Senator Heitkamp had meant by that. Yes, politics is tough—isn't that what she'd signed up for? Gun control was certainly a "tough" issue, but it was also a vitally important one.

Heitkamp had said that most of the callers to her office had been opposed to the background check bill, but that wasn't a convincing argument. Gabby had been in politics long enough to know that phone calls are usually an indicator of passion and intensity—but little else. They don't accurately measure the public's support for a piece of legislation and should never be confused with a poll.

"What are we going to do with these people, Gabby?" I asked.

She just shook her head but didn't say anything.

* * *

We had made a push during lunch that day at the Democratic caucus. New Jersey's Frank Lautenberg was too ill to make it, but every other Democrat attended. Gabby sat next to Senator Dick Durbin. Four Democrats who said they would not support Manchin-Toomey were in the room: Heitkamp, Alaska's Mark Begich, Mark Pryor from Arkansas, and Montana's Max Baucus. We needed each one to reach our magic number, 60. The Democratic leadership asked me to give a short speech about ARS's efforts. Senator Baucus walked out in the middle of my talk.

Another "no," I guessed. The math was not looking good.

After the Senate lunch, Gabby and I had a nice meeting in Joe Manchin's office with the senator, his wife, Gayle, and Senator Toomey. It was the first chance we had had to thank them for their leadership and courage.

Their bill would reduce gun violence in America, period. The Public Safety and Second Amendment Rights Protection Act required NICS background checks for gun sales at gun shows and over the Internet. It improved grants to states to encourage them to send mental health records to NICS. And, as I've said before, the bill enhanced Second Amendment rights along the way. It loosened restrictions on interstate sales, and exempted buyers with concealed-carry permits from having to pass a background check when buying from a dealer.

The NRA and the gun lobby loved to claim that the federal government was bent on creating a federal gun registry. But again, the Manchin-Toomey bill explicitly banned the federal government from doing any such thing.

As we got on the elevator down the hall from Manchin's office, reporters asked how Gabby was feeling about the next day's vote.

"Optimistic," she said.

But counting votes that night, we had a hard time making it to 60.

*   *   *

By Wednesday, the day of the vote, Gabby and I were both exhausted. We had done our best to bring people to our side.

I was angry. I couldn't sleep. My conversations with senators kept replaying in my head.

"Why do these politicians come to Washington?" I asked. "To be scared by the NRA? Think about those first graders when Adam Lanza burst into their classroom. *That's* scared."

After giving a speech together at a health care company's annual meeting, Gabby's and my itineraries diverged. She would stay in Washington to monitor the vote in the Senate, while I was headed to Dover, Delaware, to testify before a state senate committee.

The governor of Delaware, Jack Markell, had invited us to come up to speak before the state Senate. An important background-check bill was being debated that day, and they were just a few votes short of what they needed to pass. I was happy to help.

Action on gun-violence laws had moved to statehouses across the country. Connecticut, Colorado, Maryland, and New York had passed laws strengthening background checks, banning some semiautomatic weapons, and regulating large-capacity magazines. Given the roadblocks in Congress, Gabby and I understood that statehouses offered our best chance to pass laws aimed at reducing gun violence, so we had begun directing our time and resources there.

In Dover, I first met with Governor Markell. The Democrat had proposed a law that would close a loophole in state law by requiring background checks for gun transfers between private parties. Like the Manchin-Toomey legislation, the Delaware bill included many exceptions, such as transfers to immediate family members and qualified law-enforcement officers.

In testimony to a packed hearing before the Senate Judiciary Committee, I said: "We don't come to the debate on

gun violence as victims. We offer our voices as Americans."
I talked about our commitment to the Second Amendment.

"We take that right very seriously," I testified, and "we would never, ever give it up—just like Gabby would never relinquish her gun, and I would never relinquish mine. But rights demand responsibility. And this right does not extend to criminals. It does not extend to the mentally ill."

I reminded the senators that "eighty-eight percent of Delaware voters support requiring all private gun sales go through a licensed dealer and be subject to a background check."

The committee passed the tougher, new law.

"A win!" Governor Markell texted me later that day. The legislature passed the bill and Markell signed it into law in May.

* * *

In Washington, the Senate voted on the Manchin-Toomey bill as I was in Philadelphia, preparing to speak on gun violence at the University of Pennsylvania's School of Social Policy and Practice.

We followed the count—vote by vote.

Begich, Heitkamp, Pryor, and Baucus voted no. The four Democrats we needed declined to support Manchin-Toomey.

Jeff Flake voted no.

In the final tally, 54 voted in favor, 46 against. Four Republicans, including Arizona's John McCain, supported the bill. Though we achieved a majority, we failed to reach the required 60. We lost.

Patricia Maisch, our friend who had made sure Jared Loughner could not reach another magazine and reload after he shot Gabby that horrible morning in Tucson, was in the Senate gallery.

"Shame on you!" she screamed when Vice President Joe Biden read the final vote. As officers escorted Maisch from the building, she had a few choice words for the senators. "They are an embarrassment to this country, that they don't have any compassion or care for people who have been taken brutally from their families," she said. "I hate them."

*   *   *

Gabby had a quieter reaction. She and Pia Carusone watched the vote from Vice President Biden's ceremonial office inside the Capitol. New York Senator Kirsten Gillibrand, another powerful woman in Washington who had been a longtime friend of Gabby's, had joined Gabby after she had voted. Also in the room was a young veteran who had had both legs and one arm amputated during service in Afghanistan. Like many veterans, he was in favor of some reasonable changes to our gun laws, having seen firsthand how powerful weapons were—and how dangerous they could be when in the wrong hands.

Most people in the room were chatting while the vote was underway, but Gabby never took her eyes off the screen. She sat directly in front of the television, intently watching the proceedings.

After the vote had been read out, Biden joined the somber group in his office. He spent a few minutes with the veteran and then walked over to where Gabby was sitting. "I am so sorry, Gabby," he said. "This is a despicable day in the Senate." It seemed to Gabby as if Biden were personally apologizing on behalf of the body he had served in for so long.

The vice president then invited Gabby to join the presi-

221

dent in the White House. Pia and Gabby rode in the vice-presidential motorcade up Pennsylvania Avenue. Biden, in the seat next to her, offered Gabby his hopeful take on the "despicable" events of the afternoon. Sensible gun-rights measures *would* pass eventually, he told us: it wasn't a question of if but when. The country, he told her, always rejects extreme views in the end. Americans are a reasonable, responsible people, he told her—and their views will eventually win out.

On the lightning-quick car ride between the Capitol and the White House (just try it with no traffic!), Biden had summed up the founding principles of Americans for Responsible Solutions.

* * *

One minute Gabby was inside the Capitol; eight minutes later, she was inside the West Wing. In the Roosevelt Room, she and Biden joined several Sandy Hook families who had gathered there. Every single person in the room was in tears. It was an incredibly emotional moment.

Gabby said that she felt personally guilty for the failure of the vote that afternoon—not because she hadn't tried her hardest to get the measures passed, but because Congress, a body she had once served in proudly, had failed these families.

After a few minutes, the outraged president came in and talked for a little while about the details of the proposal that had been defeated. But mostly, he apologized for the dysfunction and the cowardice of the Senate. He assured them that the fight would go on, and that he would never forget Sandy Hook and what those families had suffered.

Then Obama left the grieving families to make a statement in the Rose Garden with some of the Newtown family members and Gabby by his side.

The president thanked Manchin and Toomey for their "courage" in crafting such a strong compromise bill that, as he put it, "represented progress. It represented moderation and common sense. That's why ninety percent of the American people supported it."

Obama was candid about the reasons for the bill's failure. "But instead of supporting this compromise, the gun lobby and its allies willfully lied about the bill," he said. "They claimed it would create some sort of Big Brother gun registry, even though the bill did the opposite."

Though, as Obama pointed out repeatedly, "Ninety percent of Americans support universal background checks that make it harder for a dangerous person to buy a gun," the NRA had "willfully lied about the bill," distorting the provisions of Manchin-Toomey for its own ends.

"There were no coherent arguments as to why we couldn't do this," Obama said. "It came down to politics—the worry that that vocal minority of gun owners would come after them in future elections."

Obama called the vote "just round one" and said, "So all in all, this was a pretty shameful day for Washington."

In a fiery *New York Times* op-ed titled "A Senate in the Gun Lobby's Grip," Gabby shamed the senators who voted against the bill. Braced for defeat, she and her staff had written an op-ed calling out these senators for their "cowardice." The *Times* posted it right after the vote.

"I'm furious," Gabby wrote. "I will not rest until we have righted the wrong these senators have done, and until we have changed our laws so we can look parents in the face and say: We are trying to keep your children safe. We can-

223

not allow the status quo—desperately protected by the gun lobby so that they can make more money by spreading fear and misinformation—to go on."

Gabby asked mothers to stop these senators at the grocery store and say, "You've lost my vote." She asked activists to "stop giving them money." She asked citizens to go to their offices and say: "You've disappointed me, and there will be consequences."

Gabby wrote, "Mark my words: if we cannot make our communities safer with the Congress we have now, we will use every means available to make sure we have a different Congress, one that puts communities' interests ahead of the gun lobby's.

"To do nothing while others are in danger is not the American way."

* * *

On the train ride back to Washington, my own fury was tempered, somewhat, by my dinner conversation that evening with former Pennsylvania governor Ed Rendell. In the long run, Rendell said, the loss in the Senate, however painful, might turn out to be the better outcome.

"It will shake things up," he told me.

I was certainly hopeful that the vote might shake up Americans who supported expanded background checks. Americans for Responsible Solutions intended to give this majority of voters a voice at the polls. We would make sure citizens in favor of changes to our gun laws knew which candidates supported background checks and which were controlled by the gun lobby. We would contribute to candidates who supported reasonable gun-legislation proposals, and we would work to defeat those who stood against those proposals. If changing the laws requires changing the makeup of the House and Senate, then so be it. We might get a better, stronger bill in the future.

When I arrived at our hotel after midnight, Gabby was half asleep.

"Stinks it didn't pass," I said to her.

"Yes," she said. "Stinks. Long, hard haul."

* * *

We rallied for press conferences Thursday morning. Gabby's *New York Times* essay had gone viral. Headlines in newspapers and websites worldwide trumpeted her fury.

When reporters asked for my reaction to the vote, I said: "I can explain it to you, but I can't help you understand it."

Press conferences and meetings soaked up so much of the morning that Gabby and I missed our plane back to Tucson. We had a few hours to spare until the next flight.

"What are you up for?" I asked.

Without hesitation, Gabby suggested we visit the Lincoln Memorial.

That's a lot of steps, I thought, but Gabby walked up every one. At the very top, we paused and looked back over the reflecting pool and the Washington Monument. She asked me to read the Gettysburg address. When I got to "that these dead shall not have died in vain," I stopped and added Columbine, Virginia Tech, Tucson.

"Christina Green," Gabby interjected.

I added Aurora and Newtown before I read the rest of Lincoln's address.

When it was time to go, Gabby walked down the fifty-eight steps. She was quiet and determined. She had to concentrate on every step. She took her time. She could hardly look up to see the people—more than a hundred of them—who had gathered to cheer her on from the bottom of the monument steps. When she reached the last step, the crowd erupted into applause.

She posed for photos and smiled at the nonstop comments.

"We're with you, Gabby," one woman said. "Thank you so much for your service."

"We can't believe the Senate couldn't pass the bill," another woman said.

A group of students from a North Carolina Christian academy had watched Gabby's descent. About a dozen approached and asked to take photos with her.

"We're praying for you," one of the boys said. "We are behind you. You are doing the right thing."

On Friday morning, when we settled into our seats for the plane ride home, I tweeted a photo of Gabby, paraphrasing a 1967 Martin Luther King Jr. speech, "Remembering that the moral arc of the universe is long but it bends toward justice."

CHAPTER THIRTEEN

THE WAY FORWARD

Some people might have felt defeated by the failure of Joe Manchin and Pat Toomey's legislation to strengthen background checks for gun purchasers. Those people are not Gabby Giffords.

Gabby frequently reminds me to deny the acceptance of failure. She's survived a bullet wound to the head and is constantly battling the brain injury that makes speaking so difficult. Even so, every single day she counts victories, small and large. As an astronaut, I commanded space shuttle missions where failure could lead to catastrophe. We would not give up.

While Gabby and I were angered by the Senate's lack of courage, we were also energized by the outcome. In an extremely short time, we had already seen extraordinary progress. The Senate had come within a handful of votes of passing Manchin-Toomey. We had, in fact, won a simple majority in the Senate, but we needed 60 votes, not 50. In the process of lobbying for the legislation, Gabby and I had cemented connections with friends, like Vice President Biden, and forged new allies in Senators Manchin and Toomey. We saw the Senate vote as a starting point, rather than as a setback.

And there were encouraging signs all over the place. In the months since Newtown, the issue of gun violence had taken center stage in Washington. Everywhere we looked, we found evidence that reasonable Americans—including reasonable gun owners, just like us—were tired of seeing the NRA steamroll the will of the people.

But, as the defeat of Manchin-Toomey indicated, laws can be slower to change than public opinion. I've always compared this process to turning a ship around: it takes a lot of effort, and it doesn't happen overnight. But inch by inch, minute by minute, that ship will eventually change course, and the same is true of the laws of the land.

Once the country's opinion has shifted on an issue, the laws will inevitably follow. Nine out of ten Americans—an overwhelming majority—support expanding background checks to all commercial gun sales, and so Congress *will* eventually pass laws to keep guns out of the hands of criminals and the dangerously mentally ill.

And judging by the support for Americans for Responsible Solutions, we aren't alone in feeling the urgency of this issue. Six months after our launch, we had built an organization with more than five hundred thousand active supporters and raised more than $11 million.

Our message—that you can be both pro-gun and pro-commonsense safety measures—was clearly resonating all over the country. Gabby and I are proud gun owners, and we believe strongly in the right to bear arms spelled out in the Second Amendment. But we also agree with the majority of Americans who feel there are ways to protect people from the daily toll of gun violence and the mass killings that plague our nation. In founding ARS, Gabby and I were determined to show people that, whatever the NRA claims, we *can* have it both ways. It is possible to defend the Second Amendment and at the same time enact laws that keep weapons out of the hands of people with criminal, violent, or evil intent.

* * *

Still, after the Senate defeat, Gabby and I felt that the debate over guns had reached a toxic stalemate. On one side, some gun owners believe that any effort to regulate gun ownership will lead to confiscation. On the other side, many advocates would prefer guns be highly regulated. Our goal had always been to find points of agreement between these two groups, to bridge the gap between people who were not communicating on the crucial issues around gun violence, starting with the need for stronger background checks.

In the summer of 2013, Gabby and I hit the road to talk to people from all over the country for their views on this issue. We called our weeklong trip the Rights and Responsibilities tour, and we focused on states with a strong history of gun ownership, like Nevada; states whose senators had voted against stronger background checks, like North Dakota; and states whose senators had courageously opposed the party line to support Manchin-Toomey, like Maine.

Our primary objective on the seven-day, seven-state tour was simple: to start a nationwide conversation about gun violence. Gabby and I hoped to find common cause with Americans who wanted to work toward more reasonable gun laws. We also wanted to visit ranges and get in some target practice with people who like to shoot guns.

We began our trip in Nevada, at the Clark County Shooting Complex just outside of Vegas—the largest gun range in the world, where my wife planned to practice target shooting for the first time since being shot. I worried that Gab-

229

by's impaired eyesight might affect her aim. Before she was wounded in Tucson, she had been a decent shot. She used to shoot with her right hand; now she had been a lefty for more than two years. She practiced holding and aiming a .22. Her left arm was strong and her aim looked fairly decent. I had to admit I was impressed.

That morning at the shooting complex, I handed Gabby a loaded .22. Her right arm was snug in her brace. She wore hearing and eye protection. She raised her left arm, took aim, squeezed the trigger—and just like that she hit the target. It wasn't a bull's-eye, but it wasn't on the edge of the paper, either. She took a few more shots and then set the gun down.

Not bad for her first trip back to the range in two and a half years. She did as well, if not better, than I could have with my left hand.

* * *

As we zigzagged all over the country that week, we met people whose lives had been shattered by gun violence. We met proud gun owners who were upset that people with documented mental illnesses could so easily get access to firearms. We even had productive conversations with people who came to our events as protesters but left seeing that we might share some common ground after all. I might even have changed a few minds. I know Gabby did.

Perhaps the most instructive stop on our tour came in Alaska, which has a rate of gun deaths nearly twice the national average, and more suicides by gun than any other state. A recent poll had found that 72 percent of Alaska voters support background checks on all gun sales—and yet Senator Mark Begich had been among the four Democratic senators to vote against Manchin-Toomey.

Alaska's epidemic of gun violence was one reason we visited the state, and we gathered great insights into the complexity of the issue during our time in Anchorage. One morning we brought Tom Begich, the brother of Senator Begich (who was on vacation on an Alaskan island during our visit), to a private shooting club northeast of the city. Our host was Anders Gustafson, a wonderful young man who worked as a hunting and fishing guide in remote parts of Alaska. Anders brought a wide selection of his own firearms, including a 30-06 rifle and a .45 caliber pistol. We shot a few of his weapons and some of mine and swapped stories about space launches and caribou hunts.

But I received a sobering e-mail from Anders soon after we got back to Tucson. After writing how much he had enjoyed meeting Gabby and me, Anders told me that the shooting club had expelled him as a member, in part because he had taken our group there.

To me, Anders's expulsion was one of the most important but painful lessons of our tour. The polarization that occurred on the edges of the gun-violence debate was a real obstacle to progress. We *must* reach common ground with people who respect guns as we do, even if they reflexively oppose us at first. To change the tone of the conversations we're having about gun laws, we have to communicate with leaders of gun clubs, hunting organizations, target ranges—everyone who loves to shoot. I would wager that almost all of us share the same values and concerns over gun violence and safety.

Another telling incident in Anchorage occurred at a community meeting. One of the participants, a gun-store owner, stood up and repeated the standard NRA line that background checks will lead to a national registry, which will lead to government agents going door to door to collect all three hundred million guns in America. I had heard this nonsense spouted hundreds of times before—it was all straight out of the NRA playbook.

The surprising part came afterward, when the meeting was over. The gun-store owner took me aside and privately confided that he agreed with Gabby and me on extending background checks to the Internet and gun shows. He couldn't admit that in public, he said, because the NRA would call for a boycott of his store, which obviously he couldn't afford.

I shook my head in amazement. Of course. The NRA was muzzling the reasonable people and silencing any real possibility of discussion and debate.

That had to change.

* * *

Gabby and I rounded out the tour with productive stops in North Dakota, New Hampshire, Ohio, Maine, and North Carolina. We returned home to Tucson utterly convinced that now was the time to stop giving in to intimidation and start doing what's right for our country. We were well positioned right in the center of the debate.

We'd learned a great deal on our trip. In talking to both supporters and detractors, we found much misinformation on both sides. We also realized that in many cases, people were talking past one another instead of listening. We listened, and in listening we hoped to get the warring sides to hear each other, and perhaps arrive at some shared values.

In Washington, DC, as we worked to convince senators to strengthen background checks, we cited polls showing that the majority of Americans supported such laws. On our tour, we saw the faces behind the poll numbers, and we felt more hopeful than ever.

We came away strengthened in our belief that members

of Congress sometimes do not listen to their constituents as closely as they should. We met the people who voted them into office. Americans in vast numbers favor universal background checks for gun purchasers, barring criminals and the mentally ill from possessing firearms. So why isn't Congress doing anything about it?

How can we just accept the fact that the US rate of firearm-related homicide is higher than that of any other industrialized country's, according to a report by the Centers for Disease Control and Prevention? The report, requested by President Obama after the Sandy Hook shootings, said that homicide rates by guns in the US are "19.5 times higher than the rates in other high-income countries."

Though rates of gun violence are dropping, they still take a terrible toll. Day after day, innocent men, women, and children are killed or wounded by gunfire. The Bureau of Justice Statistics' National Crime Victimization Survey reported that 467,321 people were victims of a crime committed with a firearm in 2011.

This is unacceptable. As a nation, we must try to stop this violence. As Gabby and I have discovered since founding ARS, support on the reasonable side of this issue is much stronger than people—and politicians—realize. It is deep, broad, and enthusiastic.

Our Rights and Responsibilities tour gave us the perspective we needed. From coast to coast, far from the gridlock that paralyzes Washington, we found Americans who were willing to grapple with gun violence and find ways to make America safer. We came away more committed, and more hopeful, than ever.

* * *

The tour also showed us that the path to changing gun laws might be best achieved at the local level. That's where the face-to-face exchange of ideas and opinions happens best, and that's where laws often have the greatest impact. If Congress is slow to pass legislation that makes it harder for criminals and the mentally ill to get guns, then we will work on changing those laws from state to state.

With this renewed sense of purpose, Gabby and I returned from the tour more committed than ever to the mission of Americans for Responsible Solutions. We are committed to building an organization with multiple arms that will allow us to influence policy makers at every level of government— as they make their key legislative decisions and also as they plan their political campaigns. ARS is poised to serve as a force to mobilize our grassroots supporters, serve as a policy expert, lobby elected officials and their staffs, and devote resources to independent expenditure campaigns that will have an important impact on elections. We have already devoted resources to races in Colorado and Virginia, running sophisticated programs to show our support for candidates who answered their constituents' calls for stronger laws designed to prevent gun violence in their communities. We are poised to run similarly aggressive and impactful campaigns in more than a dozen races in the 2014 election cycle.

In addition to our political and policy work, ARS has established a nonprofit arm that will contribute to the public conversation about the issue of gun violence. We know that there are many important questions that must be answered in order to propel this debate forward. Some of those questions include: What are the broader costs of gun violence to our society? What costs are imposed on families, on the community, on the health care system, and on the labor pool? We need answers, and we intend to provide them.

The NRA and other gun-rights groups have certain advantages over organizations like ours. They have already been organizing for decades at the grassroots level in every state, and many of them employ ruthless strategies we would never dream of adopting for keeping their supporters in line. We never underestimate the NRA's ability to punish perceived enemies and reward friends. Without question, the NRA still ranks among the most influential advocacy groups in the country, but there's evidence that the NRA's power is on the wane.

Take the 2012 campaigns. The NRA poured a whopping $19.8 million into the presidential and congressional races. But the NRA's massive financial support for Mitt Romney failed to defeat Barack Obama. The NRA lost thirteen out of sixteen Senate races in which they were involved.

And while far too many Washington politicians continue to live in fear of the NRA's ratings, senators with low ratings—including Virginia's Tim Kaine, North Carolina's Kay Hagan, Ohio's Sherrod Brown, Missouri's Claire McCaskill, and Florida's Bill Nelson—continue to prevail in red or purple states.

And some politicians have even begun openly calling the NRA's bluff. "The NRA is just all mythology," Connecticut Senator Chris Murphy said. "The NRA doesn't win elections anymore." In August of 2013, Murphy and his fellow senator from Connecticut, Richard Blumenthal, introduced a bill that would prohibit the sale of guns and ammunition to anyone subject to a temporary restraining order and make it a federal crime for those under a temporary restraining order to possess a gun. This is a great example of the sort of legislation that people on both sides of the debate agree should become law.

With more and more Americans demanding reasonable gun laws, grassroots organizations—from ARS to the Brady Campaign, from Everytown for Gun Safety to the Coalition to Stop Gun Violence and many more—are beginning to balance the debate, shelter politicians bombarded by NRA attacks, and advocate for stronger gun-violence laws.

Political power is shifting our way.

* * *

While we work to reform gun laws, Gabby and I have continued full speed ahead in our personal lives as well. She is still dedicated to her speech therapy, and her mobility continues to improve. Every month she makes progress that impresses everyone around her. We have also grown much closer as a couple in the last few years, which I wouldn't have thought possible before. We rely on each other more for support and encouragement. We take more time to appreciate what we have and reflect on what we have lost. We spend more time considering our actions, how we can give back, and how we can make a difference. And we realize that even the most horrific tragedies can have some positive outcomes.

We've had many memorable experiences along the way. We were invited to stay aboard the USS *Carl Vinson*, best known as the ship that received Osama bin Laden's body and performed his at-sea burial, but also a ship I had landed on in the early part of my career while training to be a naval aviator. While I had spent several years of my life aboard Navy ships, for Gabby it was a first.

Gabby also attended a ceremony to commemorate the USS *Gabrielle Giffords*, a new Navy combat ship that is scheduled to be completed in 2015. And last January, my fearless wife even jumped out of an airplane—showing, by skydiving, that nothing could keep her down (even at fourteen thousand feet).

While my days orbiting Earth are done—my last space shuttle launch was in May of 2011, just four months after Gabby was shot—my twin brother Scott is preparing to spend an entire year on the International Space Station, which is the longest any American has stayed in space. This mission is also an opportunity for researchers to study how space affects the human body. Scott and I are the perfect candidates for this study because we aren't just the only siblings to have gone into space; we are identical twins. By using my brother and me as guinea pigs, researchers will be able to study the effect of long-term stays in space on genetics. I appreciate that NASA is still driven to collect data to inform future decisions that benefit our nation.

In the meantime, I get up every morning and drive my youngest daughter to school (but only sometimes, since she drives now, too), and I make fundraising calls, and I travel the country to give talks. And like Gabby, I never, ever forget what inspired us to start this organization: those twenty dead little kids in Newtown, Connecticut, who will never drive their own kids to school, or travel the country, or do any of the simple things we take for granted.

And we will no longer sit back in silence while senseless killings continue. As I said before, Gabby and I wholeheartedly agree with the NRA's belief that "guns don't kill people. People kill people." That's why we have committed ourselves to doing everything we possibly can to keep the guns out of the hands of the people who shouldn't have them.

So let's work to pass stronger laws that prevent gun trafficking, and let's make universal background checks a reality. Let's close the loopholes on gun-show and Internet sales, and strengthen laws to keep guns away from domestic abusers with restraining orders filed against them. Let's improve the federal mental health databases so that Americans who struggle with dangerous mental illnesses—who have been involuntarily committed to psychiatric facilities or ruled a danger to themselves or others—are prohibited from purchasing firearms.

These are all commonsense, middle-of-the-road measures, and every single one of them will save innocent lives.

Gabby and I are proud gun owners and protectors of the Second Amendment's right to bear arms. We can own guns for self-protection, to hunt, as a hobby, as a cherished memento from a family member. We also believe that responsibilities come with those rights. Nothing that Gabby and I advocate would infringe on them.

So we need your support. You can join us by becoming a member of Americans for Responsible Solutions. Make your voice heard. Let your elected and public officials know how you feel about gun violence. Write to your representatives and senators in support of background checks. Show up at public events. Press for answers on crucial issues such as assault weapons, high-capacity magazines, and gun trafficking.

You can tap into Americans for Responsible Solutions on our website: responsiblesolutions.org.

Tell us your personal stories of how gun violence affected your life. Speak out in your community. The time has come to take action. As Gabby says: "Enough."

ACKNOWLEDGMENTS

Telling this story is in some small way a step in a process of recovery and an attempt to make sense of the daily gun violence we are now all too familiar with. Before Gabby was injured, we didn't often think about the death toll in our country from gun violence. But after Gabby was injured and six of her constituents were murdered, it was something that we became much closer to. The massacre at Sandy Hook Elementary School pushed us over the edge and set us on a road where we would work with concerned citizens and responsible gun owners to get our elected leaders to take action.

Gabby's career in public office was built on the foundational belief that even in an increasingly divided political environment, Americans have more in common than we think—and that solutions to our nation's most entrenched challenges can be found if we put aside short-term political gains for the good of our collective futures. We realized early on that this would be an uphill battle, but we are joined by many passionate people who aren't afraid to stand up for what is right. Like Vice President Joe Biden, Republican Senators Pat Toomey, John McCain, Susan Collins, and Mark Kirk; and Democratic Senators Joe Manchin, Mary Landrieu, Kay Hagan, and Mark Udall. Gabby and I want to thank each of them and the many other committed public servants at all levels of government who work to address our nation's gun-violence problem. And we often think about people we've met along the way from all kinds of backgrounds who have helped us understand their relationship with firearms: protesters in upstate New York, the many gun-show operators and gun-shop owners we've had the chance to meet, and even hunting guides in Alaska like Anders Gustafson, whom I look forward to seeing again and joining on a hunting or fishing trip. We want to thank them for their time and effort in educating us on this issue.

We also want to thank our staff at Americans for Responsible Solutions, who are working incredibly hard each and every day to make this country a safer and more sane place. They are an incredibly talented group: Pia Carusone, Hayley Zachary, Peter Ambler, Jen Bluestein, Miri Cypers, Mary Jeanne Harwood, Isabelle James, Zak Kozberg, Patrick McConville, Megan Nashban, Mark Prentice, Ashley Nash-Hahn, Lindsey Parker, Audrey Schlette, Brittni Storrs, Tim Tagaris, Trevor Thomas, and Kaitlyn Unger. We also want to thank Harry Jaffe and Laura Moser for their time and effort in helping us write this book. It is a process, and, to be honest, one that my twenty-five-year career in the Navy and at NASA didn't adequately prepare me to do.

We often feel like we are standing at the bottom of Mt. Everest looking up. But with the strength and determination of the hundreds of thousands of people who have joined us, we will reach the summit. So above all, we want to thank each and every one of you. We can and will find a way to bring common sense back to this issue and, most important, save lives.